Paddy Chayefsky, who built for himself a first-rank reputation as a television dramatist, turns his full attention to film writing with his first original screenplay, THE GODDESS. Here is the complete text and working script.

THE GODDESS tells of a life cycle. It is about a girl who realizes her adolescent dream—the great American dream —of becoming a movie star. She is a child of the depression; her mother wishes to be free of her; she grows up and ends up incapable of love. The play traces her background and her circuitous rise in Hollywood. It follows her into her eventual and inevitable private life—lonely, desperate, eccentric—and into an ironic echo of her mother's failure.

Chayefsky brings to THE GODDESS all the perception, compassion and skill that have made him one of our outstanding dramatic writers, and creates a work deeply concerned with the nature of our generation.

Also by Paddy Chayefsky:

TELEVISION PLAYS

THE MIDDLE OF THE NIGHT

THE GODDESS

A SCREENPLAY BY

Paddy Chayefsky

SIMON AND SCHUSTER · NEW YORK · 1958

LIBRARY OF CONGRESS CATALOG CARD NUMBER: 58-7514
MANUFACTURED IN THE UNITED STATES OF AMERICA
BY H. WOLFF, NEW YORK, N. Y.

For Sue

CONTENTS

PREFACE

IT IS A LOT HARDER *to make a good movie than you might think. I use the word "good" here quite advisedly. What I really mean is an "art" film, but I would rather avoid any discussion on what is art and what isn't. I don't really care what art is as long as it happens. To me, art is simply the work that an artist produces, and an artist is a man who creates for the single purpose of satisfying himself. An "art" film, then, is a picture made by artists because this is the kind of movie they themselves would like to see.*

The thing about an art film that most intelligent people forget, however, is that like any other film it is expected to make a profit. If the producer of an art film does not make a profit he will not be given the chance to produce any more films, art or otherwise, and a lot of good his aestheticism will do him then. All artists work for this inexorable governor of profit, not just movie-makers. The poet writes a poem with the intention of publishing it, and the painter hopes to see his work hung in a good gallery. The only difference between movie-making and any other art is that it is more difficult to make a profit from a movie.

You just can't simply go out with your 16-mm Bell and Howell and shoot a feature film, let alone a good one, and least of all a film with artistic pretensions. The cheesiest movie production will have fifty people on its payroll, and probably closer to a hundred. You have to rent studio space, build sets, buy thousands of feet of film. You have to pay union carpenters, electricians, plumbers, painters, labora-

tory men above and beyond your irreducible minimum crew of thirty-two men, your office staff, your actors, direc-tor, producer, writer, lawyers and accountants. You simply cannot make a good feature film for less than $500,000, and a budget as low as that means very few sets, very in-expensive actors, and very little location shooting. It also implies that the director, producer and writer will work for at least half a year for one fifth their usual incomes, a sacri-fice even dedicated artists are loath to make. Marty, for example, which was paid for with buttons and bones rather than money, still cost about $500,000 and probably more. The Bachelor Party, *a simple film, cost over $900,000. Now, when a film costs $900,000 to make, the piquant system of economics that governs moviemaking dictates that it will have to gross about two and a half million dollars before it will return a profit. There are huge costs that occur after the film is finished. Thousands of prints of the film have to be made; the film must be advertised and publicized. The distributor takes a large percentage of every dollar that comes in at the box office, and the individual owner of each movie theater gets his share. So a film, roughly speaking, has to gross more than twice its initial cost before it is suc-cessful. Not many films nowadays gross two and a half mil-lion dollars. I would not take too seriously the multimillion-dollar grosses claimed so often by the movie companies. This sort of exaggeration is one of the vanities of the indus-try. Even films without artistic pretensions have been gen-erally unsuccessful the past few years. The art film, however, is certainly the wildest gamble you can make.*

Producers usually hedge their investments by casting box-office names in their films. The independent entrepre-

*neur of an art film doesn't even have that security. Getting
a box-office actor is not as easy as merely submitting a good
script for the actor's consideration. For one thing, there are
very few box-office names any more, and these are not
necessarily good actors. Even if they were good actors, they
might not be right for the part, and you no longer have an
art film if you cast for box-office value rather than the spe-
cific talent. Let us say, then, that the star is a good actor
and right for the part—Marlon Brando or William Holden
or Marilyn Monroe, for example—you still can't get them.
First of all, they are committed to pictures years in advance.
Secondly, they have independent movie companies of their
own, and, instead of your hiring them, they hire you. The
same goes for Jimmy Stewart, Frank Sinatra, Gary Cooper,
Burt Lancaster, John Wayne—just about every actor who is
worth his salary at the box office.*

*So you can forget using box-office stars, and the art film
must be made, quite frankly, in the hurried, slipshod way
that any other low-budget Grade B film is made. The production of an art film is a shoestring business, demeaned by
haggling and skimpiness. The lower the budget, the more
chance of profit, so the whole idea is to keep your expenses
down. This means slicing days off your shooting schedule,
cutting out scenes that would enhance the picture but are
not dramatically vital, telescoping three sets into one. In
Marty, we gave up several delightful photographic touches
because we simply could not afford the fifty extras or the
fact that the scene would have to be shot on Sunday, which
is triple-time. You are forced to yield those elegant little
colors and gentle shadings that make the difference between
the good and the beautiful.*

Preface

In The Goddess, *we skimped nothing once we started actual production, but there were several long conferences before the first day of rehearsal whose only purpose was to cut costs. John Cromwell, the director, Milton Perlman, the producer, George Justin, the production manager, and I sat, scripts in hand, the tenor of the conference being something like this: "Do we absolutely need that big Hollywood party scene? Because it will cost a fortune to construct such an elaborate set, to rent such expensive costumes, to hire two hundred extras, and to spend one whole shooting day on this one scene." And the answer was "No, we don't absolutely need it," and the scene was cut from the script despite the fact that it would have given charm and delight to a clumsy transition. Or the assistant director, Charlie McGuire, who laid out the shooting schedule, would be instructed to "keep our Maryland location shooting down to one week, no matter what that means." It means, frankly, racing through difficult and sensitive scenes, settling for half of what you really want, eating your heart out in a frustrated fury of unfulfillment. The idea that a director shoots and reshoots a scene until he has just what he wants is palpable nonsense, especially in an art film. John Cromwell and I let a lot go by in* The Goddess *because we couldn't afford to spend any more time arguing with Kim Stanley over the nuances of her interpretation or with the cameraman to give us a more exquisitely shadowed mood in the lighting. We took what we could get as well as we could get it. Fortunately, or rather calculatedly, we had fine talents to work with. The pressure of time doesn't mean Miss Stanley isn't superb in her performance or that Arthur Ornitz, the cameraman, hasn't lighted some lovely scenes.*

The point is that an art film is never half as good as it should be. An art film must be low-budget, and low-budget means you sacrifice some art.

The trick, of course, is talent. You get a talented director and talented actors, a talented cameraman, a talented crew. A good actor can work as fast as a bad one. A good cameraman can set his lights up as fast as a bad one. A good crew is faster than a bad crew. A good production manager knows every inch of waste that can be cut without serious damage. You need imaginative propmen, inventive grips, and, above all, a morale little short of dedication. The hiring of personnel on a film is as important, if not more so, than the caliber of the script. Without a script you cannot have a picture, but without talent in every part of the show you cannot have a good picture. The Goddess is a good—an awfully good—film, I think. It is nowhere near what it could have been, for we reached for the heights with this one and we only made them occasionally. But here and there are scenes of great artistry. The first fifteen minutes of the third act are among the finest fifteen minutes of drama I have ever seen anywhere. Fifteen minutes of beauty is a proud achievement for any drama.

Well, then, so you have a good picture, even a fine piece of dramatic art, then what? What do you do with it? Now, the art is over and the problem of profit begins in earnest. The sale and distribution of any film is problematical, but an art film is the sheerest sort of gamble. You cannot put a picture starring Kim Stanley and Lloyd Bridges into the Radio City Music Hall at Easter. The Radio City Music Hall doesn't want it. You have got to play the art houses with The Goddess. This is not so simple as it sounds. There

*is only a handful of art houses in the country, and these
are all in the big cities. The term "art house" itself is not
one of esteem; it merely indicates the theater is too small
to bring back a large weekly gross, and the more expensive,
more important films don't bother playing in them. A smash
hit in the Paris Theater in New York, with crowds standing
on line for hours, can bring back $25,000 a week. You can
get a $25,000 gross in two days at the Capitol Theater with
an indifferent success. The point is, you cannot play just art
houses and gross two and a half million dollars or even half
of that. A film made for seven hundred-odd thousand, as*
The Goddess *was, must play to good audiences in 3,500
theaters. It must play as the main feature of a double bill
because for one thing it is two hours and five minutes long
and anything over an hour and a half cannot be sold as the
second feature. The exhibitors do not want four- and five-
hour programs; there isn't enough turn-over for them to
make a profit. Besides, the second feature brings very little
money to the distributor; they make all their profits on the
main feature. How do you get the proprietor of a drive-in
theater outside Joplin, Missouri, to play a long art film
starring Kim Stanley as his main feature? That is the problem of distributing art films. The art film competes with
Westerns, horror films, and big-name block-busters with
no handicaps given because your film is art and the other
might be hack. Those art films that have been hustled into
the open field have usually died a hero's death.* Twelve
Angry Men, *a genuinely good film, may conceivably turn
a small profit, mostly because of a good foreign gross.* A
Hatful of Rain *made very little profit if any at all.* A Face
in the Crowd *died ignominiously.* Baby Doll *showed a mild*

profit on the strength of unpleasant publicity rather than its own merits. John Huston pictures, for all their imaginativeness, usually collapse financially. The same is true of Orson Welles pictures.

The plain truth is that an art film must be a sensational success if it is to be a success at all. The pattern of distribution now seems to be to open an art film in one of the better-class art houses (now described as prestige houses), to hope for rave reviews, to spread the film around the big cities until considerable sales momentum and interest have been aroused, and then to let it filter down to the broad base of motion-picture selling. Every step along this path of distribution is unpredictable. Art houses are usually booked for months and are not casually accessible any time you want them. Your reviews, more likely than not, will not be raves. Critics, for some reason or another, judge a seriously intentioned film more severely than they judge a run-of-the-mill film. Since your film is art, it is by definition not lewd, and therefore you cannot promote an audience by provocative publicity and advertising, not that sensationalist advertising does really get people into the theater. (Actually, the producer has nothing to say about advertising; this is the distributor's jealously guarded province.) Whatever the case, the art producer does not want lascivious advertising, and he cannot afford any extensive publicity. So you have made a film for adults although the basic movie audience is the teen-ager; you can't afford to publicize it, and the company that is distributing your film probably has four other films they are distributing at the same time which they consider much more commercial. You cannot find a theater in which to play your film, and, on top of

*all that, you are probably deeply disappointed in the pic-
ture. Really, the man who sets out to make an art film must
be very vain, or else out of his mind.*

*Still, art films are being made, and more and more fre-
quently. The present tendency is toward the low budget.
Some of our finest writers—Arthur Miller and Tennessee
Williams and others—are trying their hands at it. It is a
wonderful medium. There is always, of course, the strong
possibility that your film will go over very well. By its very
nature, art should succeed better than hack work, because
the artist is better at his craft than the hack and his product
will be a finer one. Besides, there is no true conflict between art and commercial success. Most artists are amply
recognized in their own lifetime. In the dramatic arts especially, genuine talent shows quickly. The bizarre economic
structure of moviemaking and selling is no longer as strin-
gently confining as it was. Most distributors will tell you
they no longer know what makes for a hit film and what
makes for a flop. High-price films with name stars, like
Love in the Afternoon, may do badly in the huge Paramount
Theater in New York but still be a wild success in the Plaza
Theater, which is an art house. New techniques in selling
and distribution are being painfully worked out to deal with
a television-bound audience, and I rather suspect these techniques benefit the art film.*

*The point is that if you are an artist and if you make
a film you cannot help but make an art film. If you are good
at your craft, the odds are you will make a successful art
film. On this basis, I think, American movies can contribute
quite a bit to our innate desire for dignity in our culture. I
wrote this actually only to help make clear to those people*

who want good films just what it means to make one. And to demand a certain respect for the courage as well as the artistry of the Kazans and the Shulbergs, the Orson Welleses and the Hustons, and all the other proud men who seem determined to make good pictures.

PADDY CHAYEFSKY

THE GODDESS

Cast

EMILY ANN FAULKNER AND RITA SHAWN
                                    Kim Stanley

DUTCH SEYMOUR	Lloyd Bridges
EMILY ANN FAULKNER *(age 4)*	Chris Flanagan
THE MOTHER	Betty Lou Holland
THE AUNT	Joan Copeland
THE UNCLE	Gerald Hiken
EMILY ANN FAULKNER *(age 8)*	Patty Duke
THE BOY	Burt Brinckerhoff
THE FIRST GI	Roy Shuman
THE SECOND GI	John Lawrence
JOHN TOWER	Steve Hill
THE MINISTER	Gerald Petrarca
BRIDESMAID	Linda Soma
THE WRITER	Curt Conway
JOANNA	Joanna Linville
HILLARY	Joyce Van Patten
BURT HARRES	David White

FIRST MAN	Mike O'Dowd
SECOND MAN	Sid Raymond
LESTER BRACKMAN	Bert Freed
R. M. LUCAS	Donald McKee
MRS. WOOLSY	Margaret Brayton
MR. WOOLSY	Werner Klemperer
THE COOK	Louise Beavers
THE ELDER	Fred Herrick
THE SECRETARY	Elizabeth Wilson
THE DAUGHTER	Gail Haworth

The Goddess *was a Carnegie Production
released by* COLUMBIA PICTURES CORPORATION

Music composed and conducted by
VIRGIL THOMSON

Produced by MILTON PERLMAN
Directed by JOHN CROMWELL

The production was under the special supervision of
GEORGE JUSTIN

FADE IN. *Under the credits:* LONG SHOT *of a bus, Greyhound, vintage 1930, rolling along on a highway. It is a bright summer day. This is tobacco and farm country, long, flat fields, farmhouses. The following legend appears:*

PART ONE

Portrait of a Girl

Then, after this has faded for a moment, still on the long shot, the following legend:

BEACON CITY, MARYLAND—
1930

FADE IN *on interior of the bus.*

CLOSE TWO SHOT *of a young mother, aged 26, and her four-year-old daughter. The mother is somber, staring out of the window. The little girl is sleeping in her seat. The bus is half-filled with people whose faces are of grim demeanor.*

CLOSE SHOT *of the mother looking expressionlessly out of the window.*

MOTHER'S POV:* *A desolate farm, a broken-down deserted barn, a rusted plow or barrow projecting forlornly out of a wild tobacco field.*

MOTHER'S POV: *A deserted "loose-floor" or tobacco warehouse, windows broken or boarded up, the large front door gaping open and hanging loose on broken hinges. We see a large, crude, hand-printed sign as we rumble by. It reads:* CLOSED FOR DEPRESSION.

EXTERIOR. *Main street. Dusk.* LONG SHOT *of the bus rumbling into the main street of a fair-to-middling-sized town.*

MEDIUM SHOT: *Looking at the bus as the mother and the little girl disembark. They stand a moment, looking at the strange town. The bus pulls away.*

* Point of view. Written hereafter as POV.

MOTHER'S POV: *A row of stores, either boarded up or with broken windows. A feed shop with a large sign slashed across its window:* NO CREDIT! *Camera pans slowly. Four or five gloomy men standing morosely, incommunicatively, in front of the courthouse. Two old 1930 and older trucks, two cars, dusty and beaten, stagger down the almost empty street. A greasy hamburger joint with two men lounging silently in front of it, watching to see who gets off the bus. The Hotel Montgomery silent and grimy. A dry-cleaning shop, and then a series of indistinguishable shops, gray and listless in the gathering dusk. The stores eventually trail off into small two-story brick buildings and small white clapboard houses. In short, the main street of a Southern town of 10,000 population in 1930. The mother checks an address on a piece of paper which she has taken out of her purse, studies the numbers on the stores in front of her, and starts off down the street toward the private houses in the distance. The little girl tags after her.*

DISSOLVE TO *Interior. The uncle's home.*

WIDE SHOT *showing the little girl being held and beamed at by a pleasant-looking woman in her early thirties who is wearing a house dress. The little girl is the center of an admiring circle consisting of the woman holding her who is her aunt; a smiling but harried-looking man in his late thirties who is her uncle; and her mother. When they talk we will know that all three are Southerners. The parlor is typically lower middle-class Southern. It has a cluttered feeling, owing more to the sobriety of the furnishings than to an excess of bric-a-brac. There is a long table on which sits a series of family portraits, and a small fireplace over which sits a modest mantel. The end tables all have doilies, and there is a candy dish on each one. There is the inevitable overstuffed chair and the platform rocker, a heavy standing lamp with fringed shade and a heavy table lamp with fringed shade. The somberness is hardly relieved by a calendar with a Protestant-type religious picture on it and two or three other pictures in the temper of "Jesus in the Garden." There are a number of magazines and catalogues piled neatly on the mantel, mostly* Good Housekeeping, Sears, Roebuck *catalogues, and* The Progressive Farmer.

THE AUNT (*Bursting with enthusiasm at the little girl she holds*): Oh, she's just adorable!

THE MOTHER: Emily Ann, what do you say to your Aunt Alice when she says how pretty you are?

The mother seems abruptly to have forsaken the stony melancholia that hung over her in the preceding scenes. She is all pretty Southern belle now, eyes flashing, gay almost to the point of lightheadedness, comfortable in the flurry of formalities of visiting and being welcomed.

4

THE UNCLE: She is the spitting image of you, Lorraine!
THE MOTHER: I can't believe you never saw her before!
    Has it been that long? Wasn't you down in Mama's,
    George, when we was . . . No, you wasn't there.
    Betty Flo said you was sick. That's right, you was
    sick. Oh, my, you have a lovely home here. I sold
    my house, George. It broke my heart, but the
    creditors were hovering around us like vultures,
    and the mortgages—I don't know how many there
    was. Papa came down and handled all the details.
    We got four thousand dollars for it from a man who
    lived in Knoxville, but all that was left when we
    paid Herbert's debts was seven hundred dollars.
    Well, wasn't that just like Herbert, committing
    suicide and leaving me with so many debts I don't
    have a house any more! Oh, for heaven's sakes,
    George, don't look so alarmed. I haven't come up
    here to stay with you more than a four- or five-day
    visit.
THE UNCLE: Well, Lorraine, we fixed you up a nice
    room here and you can stay as long as you want.

*He darts a quick look at his wife, who is pointing
out things through the window for the little girl.*

THE AUNT (*From the window*): Lorraine, I'm sure you
    would like something to eat or drink or something.
THE MOTHER: Well, I been riding six hours in that bus,

and I'll tell you what I would like. I'd like a good drink of whisky—that's what I would like.

THE UNCLE (*Going to the sideboard*): Sure.

THE MOTHER (*Sinking into a soft chair, exhausted*): Mama's fine, George, and sends you her love.

THE AUNT (*Carrying the little girl to the kitchen*): I'm going to get this little girl some milk and cake.

THE MOTHER: Well, she certainly takes to you, Alice Marie. She don't readily let people hold her like that.

The aunt exits. The mother sends a quick, probing look over to her brother, who is pouring a drink for her at the sideboard.

THE MOTHER: Well, she certainly does take to Alice Marie, George. It's a pity you all never had children. I know how much Alice Marie has wanted a child. They are a joy and a mainstay in times of distress. The night that Herbert shot himself in the head I cried and I cried. And then I went upstairs and I went into Emily Ann's room, and I looked down at her sweet, sleeping face, and I was able to face the terrible burdens that were ahead of me.

THE UNCLE (*Bringing the drink to her*): We meant to come down to Herbert's funeral, but I had my jaundice, and . . .

THE MOTHER (*Takes the drink and sips it a little nervously*): I can't tell you what the five years of my

6

marriage was like. Mama said I shouldn't have married him. I could have had any number of boys. You know that, George. I thought he was going to be such a successful man. Everybody said he was a live wire. He was going to have a chain of dry-cleaning stores all through Tennessee. Oh, he was a big talker, he was. Well, he was a failure, and I told him so. He was common, and I married beneath me, and I got my proper due. Left alone with a four-year-old child, without even a nigger to help me, and a hundred and seventy-one dollars in the bank. What am I supposed to do now?

She swallows the rest of her whisky and hands the glass back for more.

THE UNCLE (*Pouring the second drink*): I could let you have a little bit of money, but there's a depression on, you know, and . . .

The mother stands, takes the second drink and smiles, the brittle façade of the lighthearted Southern belle promptly restored to her face.

THE MOTHER: Now, let's not talk about these things! My goodness, I haven't seen my own brother in five years, and this should be a joyous occasion!

DISSOLVE TO *Interior. A bedroom in the uncle's house.* CLOSE SHOT *looking across the face of little Emily*

Ann now lying in a bed but not asleep. Her eyes are wide open. The room is dark and hushed. The only light is a thin shaft coming sharply in from the second-story landing outside. A silhouette and then a second silhouette pass across the slightly open doorway, momentarily blacking out the light. The little girl's head turns to see what it was.

INTERIOR. *Landing outside the bedroom.* MEDIUM SHOT *of the uncle and the aunt at the top of the stairs leading down to the first floor. The uncle has already started down the stairs but is being kept from going any farther by his wife's desire for a whispered conference. The uncle has the air of having gone through this particular conference a thousand times.*

THE UNCLE (*Heavy whisper, containing his irritation*): I don't know what she wants, Ellie. She says she don't want any money. She says she don't want to live with us. I don't know what she wants.

They stand a moment, at the head of the stairs, silent, frowning, anxious, and then the uncle starts down the stairs. A moment later, the aunt follows him. Three quarters of the way down the narrow staircase there is a closed door which the uncle opens.

THE AUNT: Might as well leave the door open, George. Let the heat up.

8

They continue out of sight past the door. Camera pulls back so as to see the bedroom door, which opens, and the little girl cautiously pads barefoot onto the upper landing. She stands at the head of the dark, narrow stairs trying to look down. She wears a cotton nightie.

INTERIOR. *The parlor of the uncle's house. The mother, wearing a flouncy Southern-belle-type dress, is at the mantel looking at a pile of magazines on a table. The uncle is seated heavily, still frowning, in his soft chair. The aunt perches watchfully on the edge of the mohair davenport. Through the chintz-curtained window, we see it is dark night out.*

THE MOTHER: Don't you have no movie magazines, Alice Marie? Is all you got *The Progressive Farmer?*
THE AUNT: I tucked your little girl in and—
THE MOTHER *(Straightening):* Well, she certainly takes to you, Alice Marie. She is absolutely crazy about you. I never did see her take to anybody like she takes to you.

She moves restlessly around the room, frowning at the pictures of Jesus on the wall, the radio with its gaping speaker, the endless Georgian moldings on the wall, all the while the bright toothy smile fixed on her face.

9

THE MOTHER: Well, I must say that was a wonderful dinner. George, Alice Marie has made a wonderful home for you.

THE AUNT: Oh, come on in the kitchen. What we sitting out here in the parlor for?

THE MOTHER: I always envied girls who can cook because I am dreadful in the kitchen. I am sort of gay and giddy, but that's my nature, smiling in the face of adversity. Can I turn the radio on?

The question is rhetorical; she has already done so.

THE AUNT: Go right ahead, Lorraine.

THE MOTHER: I can't remember the last time I went dancing. I can't remember the last time I did anything.

A razz-ma-tazz orchestra suddenly bursts out from the radio, playing "Exactly Like You," and the mother hurriedly bends to lower the volume.

THE MOTHER: I do think I kept my figure, don't you think so, Alice Marie?

THE AUNT: You don't look more than nineteen years old, Lorraine.

The mother dances a step or two of fox trot. She is nervous, restless, fidgety.

THE MOTHER: If I have a fault, it's I'm a little vain. I was anxious about my figure after Emily Ann was born, but I assiduously did exercises every morning, and I think everything is where it should be. I still catch an eye when I walk down a street. There was a man in the seat in front of me in the bus coming over to here that like to broke his neck trying to strike up an acquaintance. I do think I would like to get married again. What do you think a proper period of grace should be—about Herbert, I mean —before I go out seriously with a man? There is a man who I know is interested in me back in Clarksville. I don't know what else I can do except get married. I can't stand being alone! Can I please turn off the radio? It's driving me crazy!

She flicks the radio off.

THE UNCLE: Well, now, Lorraine, you just sit down and take it easy and don't be so excited.

The mother shuts her eyes, sighs and makes a visible effort to get hold of herself.

THE AUNT: Sit down, Lorraine. You have been living through a terrible ordeal.
THE MOTHER *(Distraught)*: Mama said I could come live with them in Knoxville, but she and Papa are living in that little dirty two-room apartment right

on Main Street, right over the five-and-dime store.
I would think they would die of shame living there!
I couldn't live there! And this man says he's been
in love with me for years! He's a very attractive
man. A little elderly, but attractive! I mean, five
days after we had buried Herbert, he was asking
me to marry him! I said I would think about it. He
has a very nice home. He lives there all by himself
with his sister. But he doesn't like children. *(She
stares at her sister-in-law and then at her brother)*
He says he don't want no four-year-old little girl
hanging around his neck.

*Again she stares at the two other people, wondering
if they get the point. Then, taking the bit in her mouth,
she says it:*

THE MOTHER: I was wondering, since she's absolutely
crazy about you, Alice Marie—I never saw her take
to anyone like she took to you this afternoon—so I
wonder if I could just leave her here just for a year
or so, just till I manage matters better with this
man.

THE AUNT: Lorraine, she's your own little girl!

THE MOTHER: You always said you wanted children,
but—

THE AUNT: You can't just drop her on somebody's door-
step like that, Lorraine.

THE UNCLE: Lorraine . . .

The mother fights back tears of fury and guilt, shame and confusion.

THE MOTHER *(Crying out):* I'm only twenty-six years old! I still got my figure. I want to have a little fun. I can't support her. I haven't got any money!

THE UNCLE: Maybe I could help you get a job.

THE MOTHER *(Whirling on him):* I don't want no job! I don't want no dirty job!

THE AUNT: Lorraine, honey, she's your baby.

THE MOTHER *(Whirling on the aunt—a tantrumy little girl herself):* I don't want her! I don't want her! I was seventeen hours in labor with her, and she's been trouble ever since! I didn't want her when she was born, and I don't want her now!

THE UNCLE *(Sharply):* Lorraine!

She turns away dissolved in tears, her thin shoulders shaking.

THE UNCLE *(After a moment):* Well, how about his family?

THE MOTHER: I can't go to them.

THE UNCLE *(Didn't hear her):* What?

THE MOTHER: I can't go to them.

THE UNCLE: Well, it's his kid too, Lorraine.

The mother now sits perched on the edge of the straight-back chair, her head bowed, her eyes closed against her tears.

THE MOTHER (*In a low voice*): I don't rightly think it is. (*She swallows, beyond shame now*) Well, we didn't get along almost from the beginning, and I had to do something.

She stands, in control of herself again, but unable to face the other two, who are staring down at the floor.

THE MOTHER: Well, I expect I'll have to go out and get a job or something.

She moves out of the parlor into the entrance foyer, which contains the iron hall furnace and a settee. She suddenly looks up, conscious of being watched.

MOTHER'S POV: *Looking up the dark narrow stairway leading to the second floor. Just beyond the opened door, which is about six steps up, we can make out little Emily Ann, half lighted by the upstairs landing light, hunched over peering down into the entrance foyer.*

CLOSE-UP *of Emily Ann. Her little face is expressionless, but she has heard just about everything. She turns and moves back up the stairs away from camera. We watch her till she disappears at the head of the stairs.* FADE OUT.

FADE IN *on Exterior. School playground. Day.*

HIGH ANGLE SHOT *looking down on a crowded playground of a public school on a bright June day. The place is filled with boys and girls of all ages up to fourteen, a few teachers, and the sounds of whooping it up and high childish laughter.*

CLOSER WIDE SHOT *showing Emily Ann, a pretty girl of eight, in a plain cotton dress, carrying a thin textbook and a brown envelope. She wears high ankle-support shoes and her hair is cut in the straight pageboy style of those years. She comes out of one of the doors of the school into the playground. We can now distinguish some of the words the kids are shouting at each other and to their parents. Apparently, it is promotion day, and some of the kids are comparing report cards or showing them to their teachers. We hear the following ad libs as camera slowly pans Emily Ann walking alone through the exuberance of the playground.*

"I got promoted today. You get promoted?"

"I got Miss Coyne next year. Who you got?"

"We're in the same class! Hurrah! Hurrah! Hey, Thelma Sue, Sara Anne and I, we're in the same class next year."

Etc.

CAMERA WATCHES *Emily Ann until she has made her way to the gate in the high wire fence leading to the street.*

DISSOLVE TO *Exterior. Main Street.* HIGH ANGLE SHOT *looking down the length of Main Street, somewhat more thriving than the last time we saw it. The signs of depression are gone, and the people seem more cheerful. Men in their shirt sleeves, women shopping, stores open. Way down at the far end of the street we see the little form of Emily Ann walking toward us, carrying her textbook and her brown envelope.*

INTERIOR. *The five-and-dime shop.* FULL SHOT *of Emily Ann entering and looking around. The store consists of five counters running the length of the store. There is a sixth counter in the back. All of these counters are jammed with every conceivable form of notion, knickknack and odds and ends. Each wall is piled to the ceiling with boxes and cartons. Dresses and coats hang from the ceiling, obscuring the overhead light fixtures. It is a jumbled, crowded store, yet there are only one or two customers. There are three salesladies; two of them stand leaning against one of the counters, gassing about this and that. One of these salesladies is Emily Ann's mother. She is thirty now, and hard lines have settled on her face. She uses too much rouge.*

TWO SHOT *looking across the mother and the other*

saleslady, to Emily Ann coming up the aisle toward them. The saleslady calls the mother's attention to her daughter's presence. She turns to the girl with a frown of annoyance.

THE MOTHER *(Annoyed):* What do you want, what do you want, honey?

The little girl regards her mother for a moment.

EMILY ANN: I got promoted today.
THE MOTHER: That's fine. Now you go on home.
EMILY ANN *(Proffering the envelope):* Here's my report card.
THE MOTHER: I'll look at it later. Now go on home. I told you not to come around here when I'm working.

She turns back to her colleague and starts gassing away again. The little girl turns and goes back down the aisle to the open street door and out into the street.

DISSOLVE TO *Exterior. Residential street. Day.* LONG SHOT *looking across to Emily Ann standing in the driveway of a pretty, typically Southern shingle house and calling to a friend who apparently lives here.*

EMILY ANN *(Calling to the second floor):* Sylvia! You home, Sylvia? *(No answer; pause)* Sylvia! I got promoted! I'm in Miss Cahill's class next year! *(She waits for some answer again; there is apparently nobody home)* Missus Lyons, you home? Anybody home? *(Apparently not; she waits another moment, then turns and walks away.)*

DISSOLVE TO *Exterior. Street in slum section. Day.*

LONG SHOT *looking across Emily Ann's thin back to an empty lot in which four or five Negro kids are playing. Camera pans a little bit around, just enough to see the wistful expression on Emily Ann's face as she watches them. Then she turns and walks a little farther down what seems to be a pretty ramshackle street and turns in at one of the ramshackle houses. This is one of those two-family houses in which the family on the second floor climbs an outside stairway to get to its apartment.*

FULL SHOT *of Emily Ann getting to the top of the stairs, taking a key from the window sill, opening the door, and going into the apartment. In the background we see clothes hanging on lines and other indications of the slum quality of the area.*

INTERIOR. *Emily Ann's home.* LONG SHOT *looking from kitchen through living room to the front door of the apartment as Emily Ann enters. It is a cheerless, inadequately furnished place; bare walls, sparse furni-*

ture, several religious calendars on the wall, dark, even
on this bright June afternoon. A large old white icebox
with the paint chipping off stands in the living room by
the kitchen door. The reason it isn't in the kitchen is
because the wood-burning stove lets off so much heat
it would melt all the ice. The kitchen itself is dank and
unappetizing. Worn, patchy linoleum covers the floor.
There is a tall wall cupboard known as a "safe" but
which, when opened, reveals itself to be a thinly stocked
pantry containing a few dishes and some cans and
cereal containers. An old porcelain-topped kitchen
table covered by an old oilcloth sits in the middle of the
kitchen, flanked on three sides by three different chairs
—two cane-bottom chairs and a battered straight-back
wooden relic of many another kitchen. There are dishes
in the sink, empty milk bottles, and empty beer bottles.

INTERIOR. *The kitchen of Emily Ann's home.* FULL
SHOT *of Emily Ann coming into the kitchen. She places
her book and report card on the table, goes to the icebox and opens it. Over her shoulder we see two bottles
of milk, some bread, some butter, nine bottles of beer,
and that's all. She takes the milk and bread out, goes
back to the wall pantry in the kitchen, reaches on her
tiptoes and gets out a glass, pours herself a glass of milk.
Then, taking a mouthful out of her slice of bread, she
carries her glass of milk to the table and sits down.*

LONG SHOT *studying a forlorn little girl of eight*

sitting all alone in a drab little kitchen chewing a piece of bread and holding a glass of milk. Suddenly a cat jumps into the room through the window. It is a tough, big, wild-looking alley cat. The girl sits up, startled, a little afraid. The cat prowls pantherlike around the kitchen, its tail swishing, its eyes darting quick appraisals of the little girl who sits rigid in her chair watching it. After a moment, a strangely calculating look comes over the little girl's face, and she carefully stands, wary not to frighten the cat, and moves back to the cupboard shelf where the bottle of milk still stands. The cat continues its restless patrolling of the room, on guard, muscles tensed. The little girl slowly pours some milk into a soup plate and carefully sets it on the floor, and then stands unmoving, rigid, watching. For a long moment a thick silence fills the room, the cat moving around softly. Then, almost nonchalantly, it pads to the soup plate and dips its head in. For a moment the little girl watches. Then with a swoop she seizes the cat and presses it against her face.

CLOSE SHOT *of Emily Ann, her face pressed against the torn, patchy skin of the alley cat, her eyes closed, hugging the startled, frenzied animal.*

EMILY ANN *(To the cat):* I got promoted today.

The cat leaps out of the little girl's clutches and out of the window. Camera pulls back to a MEDIUM

LONG SHOT *so that we can see the sad little girl standing in the middle of the kitchen, staring off through the window through which the cat has just jumped.*

FADE IN *on Exterior. Main Street. Day, 1942.* CLOSE SHOT *of Emily Ann, now sixteen, a pretty, full-blown young girl, walking down Main Street. Camera dollies back to a* FULL SHOT. *There is an air of wanton arrogance to her, as if she is well aware that the two men lounging in the door of the liquor shop are giving her a covertly approving eye. She wears a skirt and high heels. She holds two high-school textbooks. Her hair is swept up to the top of her head in the fashion of the day. She is too young to carry all this. Camera pans with her till she turns in at the five-and-dime store. There are three high-school boys, around seventeen, wearing slacks and tee-shirts or sports shirts that fall out over their trousers, lounging at the five-and-dime entrance. They say hello to her as she sweeps past them. Then all three snicker.*

LONG SHOT *looking past the three high-school boys into the interior of the five-and-dime store. One of the boys watches her. The second boy seems to be giving the third boy intense instructions. The third boy, a stoutish young fellow, seems a little nervous.*

INTERIOR. *The five-and-dime store.* FULL SHOT *of Emily Ann walking toward the rear of the shop—the same store her mother worked in. She throws a greeting to a middle-aged saleslady as she heads to the back of the shop.*

EMILY ANN: Good afternoon, Mrs. Kimbrough.
SALESLADY (*Without looking up*): Good afternoon, honey.

Emily Ann puts her textbooks on top of a carton in the back, turns and ambles back down the aisle. There are about four customers in the shop. Her boss, a thin, middle-aged, not thoroughly shaven man, is selling two middle-aged women some men's socks. She gives her boss a greeting.

EMILY ANN: Hiya, Mr. Rice.

Her boss nods. Emily Ann's attention is actually on the entrance of the shop where the three high-school boys are still in whispered conference.

HER POV: *Looking down the aisle to the street door where two of the boys seem to be encouraging the short, stout boy to go in. They see Emily Ann watching them, and the first two boys duck out of sight, leaving the third boy in the doorway.*

THE BOY (*Mumbling; in the doorway*): Could I see you a minute, Emily Ann?

22

EMILY ANN (*Moving down to him*): You say something to me, Lewis?

Behind them, the boss looks up, frowning at the two of them.

THE BOY (*Mumbling*): You want to go to the movies tonight?

EMILY ANN: What's playing?

THE BOY: A *Woman's Face* with Joan Crawford and Melvyn Douglas.

EMILY ANN: I saw it.

This apparently dashes the boy, who is on the verge of turning and taking flight.

THE BOY: Well, I'll see you then.

EMILY ANN: I'm surprised at you, Lewis, hanging out with James Pinckney Miller and Frank Sutton out there. You're one of the nice boys in school, from one of the better families. I mean your daddy is a doctor. I don't know what James Pinckney Miller told you about me, but I wouldn't take anything he said to be very true. I went out with him just once, and he tried all sorts of things, but he didn't get very far, so I wouldn't believe anything he or Frank Sutton said. What did they say about me?

THE BOY: They didn't say anything.

EMILY ANN: I really want to know. What did they say about me?

THE BOY: We could drive over to Hagerstown. They got three movies there. There must be one there you didn't see.

EMILY ANN: Well, I would like to go out with you, Lewis, because you're from one of the better families, but I don't like you listening to any of those stories James Pinckney Miller might tell you.

Pause. The boy is afraid to push his luck. He just waits.

EMILY ANN: Well, you know where I live, and you can call for me at seven o'clock.

THE BOY *(Anxious to get out of the store):* All right, I'll see you.

EMILY ANN: You have to call for me at my house like you'd call for any girl. And you have to wear a necktie and a jacket.

The boss turns from the two women he has been selling socks to and barks:

THE BOSS: You going to buy something, boy, or you going to stand there blocking up the door?

THE BOY: I'm going, Mr. Rice.

He turns and hurries out of the shop.

EXTERIOR. *Main Street. The boy coming out of the five-and-dime. His two friends have been waiting a few store-fronts down. The three boys congregate in a little group for a moment. The boy, Lewis, is nodding his head to let them know he's made the date. The three boys start down the street, giggling to each other over some private little lechery of their own.*

DISSOLVE TO *Exterior. Balcony outside Emily Ann's home. Dusk.* FULL SHOT *of Emily Ann standing on the upper landing of the two-story house, looking down to the street, waiting for her date to show up. It is dusk, near night, and lightning bugs flit about. She wears an inexpensive organdy dress, and, despite the rather gauche upswept hair-do, she looks extremely pretty. Behind her, sitting on rockers, are her mother and Aunt Alice Marie. Her mother is now a thin ascetic-looking religionist. She wears steel-rimmed glasses, and her face is drawn into intense sobriety. The two older women are singing with quiet sternness.*

"I come to the garden alone
 while the dew is still on the roses . . ."

EMILY ANN'S POV: *Looking down to the street as a 1942 Oldsmobile sedan pulls up to the house.* FULL SHOT *of Emily Ann starting for the stairs.*

EMILY ANN: I'll do the dishes when I get home.

THE TWO WOMEN (*Singing*): "And the words I hear falling on my ear, the voice of God discloses."

LONG SHOT *looking down from balcony, as Emily Ann reaches the bottom of the stairs and hurries down the path to the waiting sedan at the curb.*

THE TWO WOMEN (*Off screen*): "And He walks with me, and He talks with me . . ."

Emily Ann gets quickly into the sedan, closes the door after her, and the car moves off.

DISSOLVE TO *Interior. The sedan driving along. Night.* TWO SHOT *of Emily Ann and the boy, now dressed in blue suit and tie, as they drive along through the night. Through the windows of the sedan we see the quiet lights of the town's residential district for a while, fading eventually into the black silence of the open road to Hagerstown. For a moment they ride in silence, the boy a little nervous, concentrating on his driving, and Emily Ann composed, even thoughtful.*

EMILY ANN: I sewed this I'm wearing myself, you know.
THE BOY: Is that a fact?
EMILY ANN: Oh, I sew most of my clothes. I'm very good at that. I sewed the dress I wore in the show

last month when the Dramatic Club, we did *Stage Door* by George Kaufman and Edna Ferber. Was you there? It was a triumph. Everybody said that was the best show the Dramatic Club has ever done. Everybody said it was just wonderful. Thelma Doris's mother said to me she never laughed so much in her life as the way I said my lines. It was a triumph! *(She is quite excited now, turned in her seat toward him, her eyes glowing.)* That was the most wonderful evening of my life. Was you there?

THE BOY: Sure, I mean I—

EMILY ANN: Everybody just came over to me and was so nice. Miss Gillespie said I was the best girl she ever had in the Dramatic Club. Well, I was so scared. I was just saying words. I didn't know I was doing anything special. Everybody was so nice to me. I began to cry. Just all of a sudden I began to cry. Miss Gillespie, she said, "What are you crying about?" I said, "I don't know. Everybody's so nice to me." She said, "You should be happy. Tonight was a triumph for you." Well, I just couldn't stop bawling. My mother was there. She said, "What are you crying about?" I said, "I don't know." Well, I'm going to tell you, we went home, my mother and I—I just didn't want to go home at all that night. I was up in the clouds. But we finally went home, and my mother gave me a hug. And I began to cry all over again. My mother, as you might know, is a Seventh-Day Adventist, and is very pious and

severe, and she didn't even want me to be in the
play. And we don't do much hugging in our house.
I do believe that was the first hug she gave me in I
don't remember—since I was an infant, I believe.
She's a Seventh-Day Adventist, you know. She
won't work on Saturday, not even in the defense
plant down there where she's working now, in the
Goodrich Rubber Company. All of a sudden in the
last few years my mother has become very religious. She was a very pretty girl when she was
young. My Uncle George says she was the belle of
Clarksville, Tennessee. That's where I was born—
that's near Fort Donelson, where Grant won the
first Northern victory in the Civil War. Well, I
couldn't stop crying all night long. And I woke up
the next morning, I no sooner opened my eyes, and
I began bawling again. I got tears in my eyes right
now just talking about it. Isn't that the silliest thing
you ever saw?

*She dries her eyes quickly with a finger, turns back
and looks out the front windshield at the road rolling
underneath the wheels.*

EMILY ANN: That was the most wonderful night of my
life.

*The boy smiles briefly, concentrates on his driving.
A silence falls between them.*

EMILY ANN (*After a moment*): I hope you don't mind my rattling on like this. I'm well aware I have the reputation of being a real ear-bender.

THE BOY: Oh, no. I'm always happy when the girl takes over the burden of the conversation.

EMILY ANN: Well, I understand I have the reputation of carrying that burden very well.

She smiles quickly at the boy and he smiles nervously back. A sudden sweet air settles over the two kids. Emily Ann is painfully aware of the feeling.

EMILY ANN (*Suddenly smiling*): I daydream sometimes about being a movie star. I guess every girl daydreams about that. I mean, I don't think I'm so terribly pretty and all that, but they have these cosmeticians in Hollywood who make the movie stars look a lot more beautiful than they are. I mean, you ought to read some of these magazines which tell you the inside stories on some of these movie stars. I mean, most of it is all cosmetics. I do believe, however, that Ann Sheridan is just beautiful, don't you think so? Lana Turner was only seventeen when they discovered her. I daydream sometimes about that. Do you daydream about that ever?

THE BOY (*Horribly shy*): Well, no, I don't daydream about that.

A pause sits between them.

EMILY ANN: What do you daydream about?

THE BOY *(Embarrassed to blushing)*: Oh, I wouldn't even tell you.

EMILY ANN: There's nothing wrong with daydreaming.

THE BOY: Well, I daydream about girls, I guess. I don't get along well with girls and . . . *(He is suffused with embarrassment)*

EMILY ANN: Well, I have to tell you, Lewis, your fault is that you are too shy. The girls all like you, they talk about you, and—

THE BOY: They do?

EMILY ANN: Oh, sure. Saranne Searle had a case on you for months. You're a very attractive boy, Lewis. You mustn't be so shy.

If the boy weren't driving, he would close his eyes, he is so embarrassed. Emily Ann studies her fingers in her lap.

EMILY ANN: I didn't exactly have a case on you myself, but I was very pleased when you asked me to go out with you today. I'm well aware that your daddy is a doctor and that there are many people in this city who look upon my mother and myself as common. Well, before my daddy died, we lived in Clarksville, Tennessee, and my father had the dry-cleaning store, and we were well thought of. My mother had a nigger come in twice a week to help

her with the washing and ironing. We were one of
the better families. *(She has been getting angry,
and her expressive young eyes begin to flash)*
There's lots of girls here wish they had my background. I know I don't get invited to the Cotillion
and the Subdeb, and you don't know how that hurt
me! I cried for weeks! I could have killed Thelma
Doris and her mother. Supposed to be my friend.
Didn't even invite me to her sweet-sixteen party.
I begged my mother a hundred times—let's move
out of niggertown. But she's crazy about money.
She hoards it away. I don't even know where myself. She don't want to pay more than seven dollars
a month for that tacky little old three rooms we got
there. What do you think I work in Rice's five-and-
dime after school for? She won't give me a penny
to buy new clothes! I have to buy all my own
clothes. I even saved up and bought my own pub-
lic-school graduation dress, the material, and sewed
it myself. Everybody thought it was beautiful.
They thought I'd gone to Baltimore to get it! *(She
is aware she is being very angry and she subsides
a bit)* Well, I certainly have a temper, don't I?
I apologize, Lewis, for that outburst, but I feel
these things very deeply. *(She sits, her turbulent
thoughts still welling in her mind)* I don't expect
you can understand the shame and degradation
that a girl feels when she isn't invited to a sweet-
sixteen party.

THE BOY (*Essentially a very decent boy*): I do understand, Emily Ann.

She looks quickly at him and then bows her head quickly not to show the sudden welling of tears his simple sympathy has generated. The car buckets along into the night.

EMILY ANN: I ask nothing except to be treated with the simple courtesy and respect that any other girl is treated.

THE BOY: I don't think that's asking too much, Emily Ann.

She raises her head and looks at the chubby profile of the boy driving the car.

EMILY ANN: You're a very sweet boy, Lewis. I like you very much.

The sedan speeds along. Emily Ann leans back against the seat and kind of looks out the side window at the swiftly passing black landscape. A vague, drifting smile curls her lips. She seems a very pretty and nice girl at the moment.

DISSOLVE TO *Interior. A movie theater.* TWO SHOT *looking across the boy to Emily Ann, who is really enjoying the movie. She sits in the dark theater, her eyes*

*rapt with attention and her well-formed mouth slightly
open, ready to laugh. Indistinguishable words and
sounds emanate from the screen, and Emily Ann's face
contorts and follows each off-stage movement like a
little girl at a puppet show. Something on the screen
produces a laugh from the audience and a fit of giggles
from Emily Ann. Then she suddenly erupts into a laugh
she can no longer stifle. She is having a wonderful time.
Camera pans a little so that we get a better look at the
boy. His interest is not with the picture. He has his arm
balanced on the space between the two seats he and
Emily Ann are occupying, and he is mustering his last
shred of courage to force himself to slide his arm around
the back of her chair. This decision is making him sweat.
His eyes are not looking at the screen; they are covertly
examining Emily Ann. Every now and then he pretends
to look at the screen. He finally contrives to get his arm
around the back of Emily Ann's chair, and his fingers
fall vaguely on her neck and that part of her shoulder
left exposed by the scalloped cut of the dress. Emily
Ann doesn't even notice it, but the boy's face would indicate he had his hand in a flame. His chin trembles and
his forehead is coated with sweat. He catches his breath
as if he had run the twenty miles from their home town.
Emily Ann and the audience suddenly burst into laughter again. The boy just sits.*

DISSOLVE TO *Interior. The sedan driving home.
Night.* TWO SHOT *of Emily Ann and the boy driving*

home. Emily Ann is still bubbling over the show. The boy's face is set in rigid determination. Through the windows of the car we can perhaps tell that we are on open highway, and only an occasional gas-station light interrupts the black flow of the wooded areas along the road.

EMILY ANN *(Bubbling with good humor):* Her real name isn't Ginger Rogers, you know. Her real name is Virginia McMath, and you know how she got started? She used to dance in Charleston contests, and somebody saw her, and that's how she became a star. I was thinking of taking dancing lessons, tap dancing and things like that, but they don't even have any place there in Hagerstown where they teach that. Do you know of any? Lana Turner was discovered in a drugstore, and there was one star— I think it was Priscilla Lane or Carole Landis—was just an old secretary, and she was riding up in the elevator, and this producer saw her and that's how she got her start. But I was talking about Ginger Rogers. I mean, she ain't like some of them stars. She don't go out to night clubs much, although there was one time there everybody thought she was going to marry Howard Hughes—it was in all the magazines. Anyway, she lives in a lovely home in Beverly Hills with her mother. She keeps her mother right there with her. I think that's nice.

Ginger Rogers' dressing room has mirrors on the ceiling and the walls, and she has fruitwood furniture, and she loves classical music, you know? She's very close with Deems Taylor. He's a well-known classical musician. She has his picture on her wall, but there's no romance there in the wind, I don't think—just good friends. *(She has suddenly become aware that the boy is turning the car into a side road.)* Where are we going, Lewis?

The boy says nothing, afraid actually to trust his voice. The road they are on now is not too well paved, and the sedan jostles and bumps. She abruptly and surely knows what the boy is up to and it stings her sharply. The bubbling enthusiasm flips off her face to be replaced by an eye-narrowed coldness.

EMILY ANN: I think, Lewis, you ought to just turn this car around and take me home.

The boy's only answer is to pull over to the side of the road, foliage and fallen branches crackling under the wheels.

EMILY ANN: Them stories that James Pinckney Miller and all the other boys may have told you are not true!

The car is stopped now, but the boy just sits staring at the steering wheel, mustering his courage again, a short, stout boy, brow beaded with sweat. For a moment they are both almost on the verge of tears, sitting stiffly, rigidly, the silence sick and tense between them. Then abruptly the boy reaches for her, twisting his stout torso past the steering wheel, clumsily trying to get both arms around her, frantically trying to put his face next to hers. Emily Ann fends him off easily.

EMILY ANN: Leave me alone!

The boy, utterly shattered, twists back behind the steering wheel. It is all he can do to keep from crying. Emily Ann sits in numb fury.

THE BOY (*Sick with shame and guilt*): You do it for all the other boys. What's the matter with me?
EMILY ANN (*Head down*): I just as soon be dead. I know what everybody thinks of me, all the boys whispering about me when I walk in the school. I'm afraid not to let them, that's all. I wouldn't get no dates at all if I didn't let them. Please take me home, Lewis. I just as soon be dead, and that's the truth.

The boy is actually deeply touched, but he doesn't know what to say. He starts the motor and shifts into first gear.

LONG SHOT *of the sedan pulling across the road and backing as it prepares to reverse direction and head back the way it came.*

DISSOLVE TO *Exterior. Street outside Emily Ann's home. Night.* LONG SHOT *of the sedan coming down the street and wheeling to a halt in front of Emily Ann's house. It is around midnight, and the street is dark except for one lone light in some distant house. The shabby little homes are outlined vaguely against the murky sky.*

INTERIOR. *The sedan.* TWO SHOT *of Emily Ann and the boy just sitting, he before the steering wheel, she against the door on her side. They have nothing to say but seem to feel something should be said. Emily Ann is too hurt to conceal the deep pain of her life from showing on her pretty, young, overrouged face.*

EMILY ANN (*Mumbling*): I would love to see you again, Lewis. I don't suppose you would care to.

The boy says nothing only because he wouldn't know how to say it. He just wants to get home and forget all about everything. Somehow Emily Ann is aware that the boy is perhaps as deeply shattered as she is. She darts a quick look at his tense face.

37

EMILY ANN (*Utter desolation*): Oh, I don't care. If you still want to, it's all right with me.

The boy looks at her, not quite sure he knows what she means. She slides over to him, spiritlessly puts her arms around his neck and kisses him in a gesture of ultimate futility. The boy cannot adjust to this for a moment, but then he seizes her almost desperately and begins kissing her on the neck.

CLOSE-UP of Emily Ann looking over the boy's shoulder. Her eyes are wide, and there are tears in them. She seems absolutely unaware of the fact that she is being made love to.

EMILY ANN (*Almost calmly*): I'm going to go to Hollywood some day, and I'm going to be a star. I'm going to be a star.

EXTERIOR. Street outside Emily Ann's home. Night. MEDIUM SHOT of the closed, dark sedan. Through the front side window we catch a vague glimpse of the two lost young kids clutched in each other's embrace, a little movement of the white of his shirt, of the light pastel of her dress. Camera pans away from the car across the unpaved sidewalk along the wall of Emily Ann's building to the upper landing.

CLOSE SHOT of the mother, still sitting on her rocker on the balcony in her faded print dress. The aunt has gone. The mother sits alone, singing almost inaudibly to herself.

THE MOTHER: "And He walks with me and He talks with me . . ."

FADE OUT.

FADE IN *on Exterior. Main Street. Night, 1944. Several shots looking down on Main Street again. But a marked change. We have faded in with a sharp blare of military music, which indicates what has happened to the small city of Butler, Maryland. It is an Army town now. From where we sit, the sidewalks look jammed with GIs, meandering, lounging, clogging up store doorways, looking into shop windows. They are lined up outside the movie house. There is a lot of weekend-pass high spirits. Underneath this, the martial music keeps drumming and fifing up a storm.*

EXTERIOR. *Street off Main Street. Night.* LONG SHOT *looking down the street that joins Main Street at right angles. It is essentially a quiet street with a little cluster of stores where it joins Main Street. The stores are closed now, and the street is dark. Way down on Main Street, we can still see a few lights. It is drizzling.*

CLOSE SHOT *looking down on a tall young GI sprawled on the wet street, one leg and one arm up on the curb. His eyes are closed, but an occasional movement shows he is alive. His face, his uniform are drenched with rain and smeared with mud, and the drizzle beats lightly down on his face. Camera slowly looks up to a* LONG MEDIUM SHOT *looking down the sidewalk to Main Street. A group of four people come hurrying around the corner from Main Street. They are two GIs and two girls. The GIs have their jacket collars up, and the two girls have found impromptu protection against the rain, a newspaper or magazine. They are walking quickly, a giggly, laughing, whispery little group. We may possibly recognize Emily Ann as one of the girls. She is now eighteen, full, sensual, wearing a light fall topcoat and high-heeled wedgies.*

MEDIUM SHOT *with the body of the drunken GI sprawled on the street in foreground as the four young people approach. The boy with Emily Ann has his arm around her. The first GI becomes aware of something in the street. A few steps later, he recognizes the form to be a GI. He slows his walk as he approaches.*

FIRST GI: Hey, look at that.

The others are also aware of the body in the street now. The girl with Emily Ann is frightened and hangs back, but Emily Ann is fascinated. She edges forward with the two GIs, who are now coming to make a closer examination of the body.

FIRST GI: Boy, he's loaded, huh?
SECOND GI: Maybe he's dead.

The body on the street moves slightly now, reliev-
ing everybody of this possibility. Behind the two GIs we
can see Emily Ann, a few steps back, watching, fasci-
nated, and the other girl even farther back. The two
GIs stand regarding the form, a little at a loss for what
to do.

FIRST GI: We ought to get him somewhere. He'll get
    pneumonia.
SECOND GI: Yeah.

He squats down beside the body, lifts the head.

SECOND GI *(To the head):* Hey, Mac.
FIRST GI *(Squatting down; impressed):* You know who
    that is? That's Tower, "E" Company. John Tower.
    (To Emily Ann) You know who this is? This is John
    Tower, the son of the movie star. Oh, what a luna-
    tic this guy is!

Emily Ann is quite impressed. She stares at the thin,
gaunt, wet face; young Tower is being helped to his feet
with great difficulty by the second GI.

SECOND GI *(To first GI):* Give me a hand with this, will
    you?

THE GIRL *(In background):* Is he all right?

EMILY ANN *(Turning to the girl ten steps or so back):*
Lucy, that's John Tower, the son of the movie star.

THE GIRL: Is he dead?

*The movie star's son hangs limply between the two
GIs. We see that he is a tall, thin boy of twenty-five.
Water streaks down the gaunt face. His eyes are closed;
he is out cold. The first GI has been digging into Tower's
pocket.*

FIRST GI: He's got a hotel key here.

EMILY ANN: Lucy, that's the son of John Tower, the
movie star.

DISSOLVE TO *Interior. The hotel room. Night.* ME-
DIUM SHOT *looking across the room to the open doorway
through which the two GIs, holding young Tower, and
Emily Ann have entered. The other girl can possibly be
seen in the corridor outside. The room is dark, and the
only light for a moment is the diffuse shaft of light pouring weakly in from the hallway. Everybody is a silhouette for a moment. Then somebody turns on the
light and the room is filled with a vague, fitful sort of
light coming from a naked and inadequate bulb hanging overhead. We can see, however, that the second GI
has managed to get Tower over to the bed, where he
lets him down. Tower slides back onto the bed, his feet
dangling over the side. He is awake, but almost coma-*

*tose. He is mumbling "Get out of here" over and over
again so that the words are indistinguishable and the
effect is gibberish. His face and hair are matted with the
filth of the street he was lying in, and the front of his
uniform is drenched through in ugly splotches of wet.
Black rivulets run off onto the wildly rumpled white
sheets. The bed is in great disorder. It is an old-fashioned brass bed. The room itself is the inevitably dreary
room of all small hotels, with faded wallpaper, a stained
washbasin in the corner (the towel is lying in a heap on
the floor), a cheap mahogany chest of drawers topped
by a cracked mirror, and a worn soft chair with a hole
in its slipcover. The first GI is standing by the wall
switch; it was he who turned on the light. Emily Ann
stands framed in the open doorway, watching the pro-
ceedings with wide-eyed fascination. She has never seen
anybody so drunk, and the son of a well-known movie
star at that. The second GI lifts Tower's feet onto the
bed with no apparent concern for the fact that the sop-
ping-wet GI's shoes are smearing the disarrayed spread.
Three empty fifths of whisky and a half-empty gallon
jug of wine are on the floor in various locations.*

First GI: What are we going to do with him, because
    it's almost twelve o'clock? We got to get to the bus,
    boy. Why don't we tell the desk clerk to send up a
    doctor or something? (*Turning to Emily Ann*) Lis-
    ten, honey, I'm sorry, but we got to make the bus,
    so you girls will have to get home alone.

EMILY ANN: Oh, don't worry about me, honey.

SECOND GI *(To the other girl, now in the doorway):* You girls can get home alone, can't you?

EMILY ANN: Oh, you boys go run get your bus. I'll take care of this boy.

The second GI has already gone out into the corridor. The first GI follows him.

FIRST GI: I'll call you during the week, honey.

EMILY ANN: That's fine, honey.

He exits. Emily Ann goes to the doorway.

EMILY ANN *(To Lucy, who has moved off):* Lucy, I'll stay here a couple of minutes, take care of this boy, take off his shoes—you know. You go on home, honey.

On the bed, young Tower lies limp and unmoving, his eyes open and staring without seeing up to the ceiling above him. Emily Ann closes the door and turns to him. She regards him for a moment, then moves quickly across the room to where the towel is lying on the floor, picks it up, and comes back to the bed where he is lying, muttering over and over again:

TOWER *(Mumbling):* Get out of here get out of here get out of here get out of here . . .

She regards him for a moment, and then bends down and begins drying his hair and face.

Quick dissolve to *Interior. The hotel room.* Wide shot *of the room, showing Emily Ann sitting in the soft chair, uncomfortably asleep, and young Tower on the bed, sleeping fitfully. The sheets are twisted around him, and his thin arms and shoulders make sudden involuntary twists and jerks. He is wearing only a tee-shirt and the trousers now. The window by the bed shows that it is dawn now, a gray-black dawn hanging sullenly over the roofs of the town. The slight persistent drizzle continues. With a sudden start he is awake. He sits bolt upright, as if he has been startled awake by a nightmare.*

Close shot *of young Tower, his face and body rigid, eyes wide. Then the terror goes, and he remains haggard, disheveled, and soddenly drunk. He slides off the bed with some creaking of the mattress, and Emily Ann opens her eyes. He crosses the room to the chest of drawers, hardly aware of Emily Ann's presence, takes one of the fifths of whisky sitting on the chest of drawers, looks around for a glass, sees it on the floor by the bed, gets it, pours himself a half tumblerful, sits down on the bed again, sipping his drink and examining his naked toes. Emily Ann watches him, wary, her face worn and exhausted. He notes her briefly. The silence unnerves Emily Ann.*

EMILY ANN: You was laying out in the street there on Jackson Street in the rain and all, so we brought you up here.

He doesn't seem to have heard her.

EMILY ANN: Are you really the son of John Tower?

She would prattle on, but in one quick gesture young Tower has sent the bottle of whisky he is holding crashing against the wall, the jagged pieces of glass spraying around, the liquor draining down the wall in small streams. Emily Ann sits petrified. Young Tower studies his glass of whisky.

TOWER (*His speech heavy and thick*): I can't even get myself a floozie without using my old man for a reference. (*He stands unsteadily and moves aimlessly around the room in his bare feet, muttering indistinguishable imprecations, his face swollen and hostile*) I had plenty of women. I don't need my father. When I was seventeen I used to steal his women. (*He turns abruptly, goes back to the bed, sits down. After a moment, he mutters quietly*) You can infer, if you wish, that I don't particularly care for my father.

Emily Ann stands a little uncertainly.

EMILY ANN *(Mumbling):* As long as you're all right . . .

TOWER: What did you say?

EMILY ANN *(Louder):* I said, I just wanted to make sure you was all right, so as long as you're all right, I guess I'll be going.

TOWER *(Stands again, unsteadily, disjointedly, looks around the room for his jacket):* Don't leave me now. I won't do anything terrible, except possibly commit suicide. That's what I came up here for, you know. Drown myself in the bathtub. Go look in there. The bath is full. I got blind as a coot last night and staggered in stark naked and fell in the tub and put my head under the water, and I almost did it. I can't describe to you the absolute tranquillity. But way back in the empty hollow some persistent hammer of life clunked away, and, at the last minute, I pulled my head up and gasped in the air and I lay on the dirty, cold, wet tiles twitching like a fish in the bottom of a boat. I just don't have the talent for suicide. I took seventeen sleeping pills in the Ashford Hotel in New York, but they rushed up the stairs with a stomach pump, and I spent the night in Bellevue. I tried gas, but all I got was color in my cheeks. I just don't have the knack. *(Suddenly leans to her)* What are you living for? Be honest now. Tell me. What's it going to add up to, this sixty, seventy years you're going to flounder around this earth? One day you'll be necking in the back of the car with one of the boys from town, and because all your friends are getting married, you'll get married. You'll put on weight, and your husband will take up with a waitress in a hotel in Chattanooga. You'll have babies and visit your in-laws in the evening, and your husband will get sick, and you'll fret about the rent. Your hair will gray, and you'll suddenly look back and say, "What happened? It's all over." Your friends will die and you'll sink into melancholic hours, sitting by a window, peering with unseeing eyes through white chintz curtains, and finally they'll drop your long wooden box into the moldering grave. And what was it all about except worry and tears? Am I lying? Isn't that it? Slings and arrows. A tale told by an idiot. Why bother? It all ends up in the grave. You might as well make an honest effort to get there.

He turns away from her and lurches back to the bed. He sits down heavily, stares with swollen, sullen red eyes at the tumbler of whisky in his hand.

TOWER: What would you know about it anyway, a frump in a hick town? You don't know what loneliness is. You think it's not having a date on Saturday night. You don't know the great, ultimate ache of desolation. I'm cold. Close the window or something.

He lies back on the bed now, staring up at the ceil-

*ing through wide, drunken, tear-filled eyes, crying
quietly and without constraint now.*

TOWER: The last time I saw my father was six years ago.
He was sitting in the living room of that barn he
has in Sherman Oaks, playing solitaire, guzzling
wine because he's too miser cheap to buy a decent
fifth of Irish whisky, half hidden behind a thin
blanket of cigarette smoke. The house was empty.
My mother had a nervous breakdown when I was
eleven. My older brother, Tom—my old man drove
him years ago into an insane asylum, where he
walks around picking up imaginary strings off the
floor. My father said, "Where have you been the
last couple of weeks?" Last couple of weeks! I had
been gone for a year and a half in the Spanish Civil
War. I said, "Pa, I need psychiatric help. I'm lost.
I have to fight sometimes to keep myself from jumping out of windows. I'm asking you to be kind to
me." He said, "I'm supporting one crazy son, and
that's enough for me." That's my old man, star of
stage, screen and radio, and a host of favorites.

*He lies on the bed, quietly, unmoving, his eyes
open.*

TOWER *(After a moment):* You wouldn't understand,
you wouldn't understand. You don't know what

loneliness means. All you ever cried at was a Street and Smith love story.

CAMERA PANS SLOWLY *to Emily Ann sitting hunched over on the soft chair. Tears make wet little paths down her cheeks. She has been quietly crying for some time.*

DISSOLVE TO *Interior. The hotel room.* MEDIUM SHOT *looking across the bed, still a tempest of sheets and spread and blankets. The sun is high in the sky now; it's a very hot noon. On the bed, a fully dressed Emily Ann and young Tower, dressed as in the previous scene, lie clutched in embrace. Emily Ann is sleeping in the young man's arms. He is awake, looking down at the full, soft young face with ineffable tenderness. The sun streams in through the window, almost whitening their faces and bleaching away the abject tawdriness of the room.*

DISSOLVE TO *Exterior. A hilly landscape. Day.* HIGH LONG SHOT *looking across the pretty countryside of Maryland with its clumps of trees and high grassy slopes, almost Renoiresque in its warm pastel charm. The sun is high and strong. Way off in the distance, but visible, we can see a soldier and a girl seated by a picnic basket.*

CLOSER LONG SHOT *looking through thickets and bushes, the sun glinting and quivering through the leaves. We can see Emily Ann and young Tower clearly enough, but they are too far away to be overheard too well. They are romping—warm, sensual, tickling, laughing, muffled, intimate enjoyment. Young Tower stands, and we can hear Emily Ann's laughter. Camera dollies in through the bracken and bramble. We see Emily Ann on her haunches gathering the wax paper and other remnants of the picnic into a pile so she can set it afire. She is laughing as she goes about this. Tower is standing, his shirt collar open, his tie dangling loosely. He is expostulating:*

TOWER: I am! I am! I'm tongue-tied, inarticulate. Silent to the point of brooding! What are you laughing at? It's true. *(He laughs)*

Emily Ann bursts into laughter again.

TOWER *(Can't resist smiling himself):* Come on!

Her laughter is too infectious; he finds himself laughing with her.

EMILY ANN: John, you haven't stopped talking since I met you.

Tower has stopped laughing and is regarding her with a quick, sudden warmth.

51

TOWER: When I was twelve years old, I was in Andover prep school. Very fancy. My father sent me to one fancy boarding school after another. I got thrown out of all of them. But when I was in Andover I knew a boy—we shared a room together —a blond boy named Elliot Sherman, and we used to sit up all night long talking about everything. He was the only boy I ever met who had read as much as I had. You can't imagine what I had read by the time I was twelve. My father had thousands and thousands of books. He bought this huge shack out in Sherman Oaks, California, and the library came with it. He never read a one of them; I read them all. Lucretius and Sophocles—all the great, desolate dramas of antiquity. I wore out Shakespeare and Macaulay and Gibbon, the fat sprawling histories of the Victorians, obscure poetry by B. V. Thompson and the elegant jaded sensuality of the Pre-Raphaelites. I used to lie all alone in the bleak, shadowed living room and read until my head fell on the books. Mark Twain. I adored him. That's all I own now are a few slim volumes of Mark Twain's black little pessimism. *Pudd'nhead Wilson's Notebook, What Is Man?,* and a collection of Eugene O'Neill, that great Irish peddler of death. I was twelve years old, mind you, and I used to stand in that empty living room quoting the sonorous despair of Edwin Arlington Robinson and the biting contempt of Jeffers. My father was out chasing

some tart, and my sixteen-year-old brother was out
wandering the streets, half demented. What a
family, huh? Well, anyway, there was this boy in
Andover when I was twelve years old, and we used
to talk all night long. And to this day, you're the
only other person I've ever talked like that with.

*Emily Ann, squatting by the little pile of refuse,
looks up at him standing beside her, and he looks down
at her, both tenuously aware that this is somehow a
declaration of love. After a moment he sits, staring at
the ground, and then sprawls on his side. She lights a
match and sets the little pile of papers in front of her
ablaze. She sits in front of the small fire and studies
her hands, nervously twitching in her lap.*

EMILY ANN (*Quietly*): I love you so much, John. I can't
tell you how much I love you. If the Army ever
stations you somewhere else, I think I'll die. I'll
follow you. I swear I will. I wish we was married.
I'll make you a good wife. I swear I will. You'll
never be sorry. Never.

*Tower rolls over on his back away from her. Emily
props herself up on an elbow.*

EMILY ANN: I'll follow you. I mean it. I will. I wish we
was married, John. I'd make you a good wife, I'll

53

make you a good home. You'll never regret it—
never.

*Tower sits up now, his back almost to her. His eyes
cloud and his features assume a rigid blandness. Emily
Ann is keenly and miserably aware of the change.*

EMILY ANN: You don't care about me at all, do you?

TOWER: That's not true.

EMILY ANN: I'm just somebody to spend the weekend
with because you can have your way with her.

TOWER: That's not true.

EMILY ANN: You keep me waiting in front of that hotel
every week, an hour, an hour and a half. I never
know if you're going to come. GIs come by, making
cracks at me till I think I'll burst. Why do I do it?
Who's he? He don't even care about me. I cry
myself to sleep every night, thinking about you. I
think about how you been hurt all your life, and
I want to take care of you and give you a good
home. And I'm just some girl for lack of any other
to you.

TOWER (*Avoiding her eyes*): That's not true, Emmy.
You're the only person I have in my life. You're very
dear to me. What do you think, I'm a big lover, I
go around scraping women off my sleeves? You're
the first girl I've talked to in months. I lie in my
barracks, so lonely I can hardly keep from getting

up and running across the street to the rec hall to call you on the phone.

She stares at him, her eyes suddenly welling with tears.

EMILY ANN: Oh, Johnny, I wish you had—I wish you had!

TOWER: I destroy everything that means anything to me. I always have.

EMILY ANN *(Furiously in love):* That's not true. I never been so happy in all my life from what you just told me.

TOWER: I'm too damaged for you, Emmy.

EMILY ANN: I want to hold you in my arms, John.

TOWER: Emmy, what are we kidding ourselves? I love you now. In half an hour I'll wonder how I ever got into this. You have a passion for respectability, and I have a horror of loneliness—that's love! See! I've destroyed it already! A sweet feeling poked its head up out of my morose solitude and I stomped it out fast. I always do. The worst thing that could happen to us is if we get married. I'd hate you before the blush of the ceremony had gone from your cheeks.

EMILY ANN: I'll make you a good wife, Johnny. I'll make you a good home.

TOWER: I love you, Emmy.

They kneel, regarding each other with deep sweetness.

DISSOLVE TO *Interior. Emily Ann's apartment.* GROUP SHOT *of a wedding ceremony, looking across the minister's back. We see Emily Ann, silent and solemn, wearing a white bridal costume and veil; young Tower, his face implacably expressionless. Around them are the mother, the aunt, the uncle in a blue woolen serge suit, two girls of Emily Ann's age dressed in cheap organdy frocks, and a GI, apparently the best man. There is a homemade wedding cake on the kitchen table which has been brought into the living room. There is also a punch bowl. The most striking aspect of this ceremony is the cheerlessness of it, the stern Baptist faces. Young Tower, in particular, seems troubled. The minister intones the service.*

DISSOLVE TO *Exterior. Outside Emily Ann's apartment. Night.* LONG SHOT *looking up to the second-floor landing. In the foreground, the wedding party of the best man, the two bridesmaids, the mother, the aunt, the uncle, either standing on the sidewalk looking up or getting into the various automobiles parked there. Three Negro kids are fascinated spectators. On the balcony stands Emily Ann, a gay, white figure. She is waving goodbye and shouting to the departing guests:*

EMILY ANN (*Shouting*): I want to thank you all very

much! I want to thank you all very much! Saranne!
I'll call you Monday morning!

THE UNCLE (*Calling back*): Don't go to sleep too late!

*This Rabelaisian advice brings a guffaw from the
aunt and a giggle from one of the bridesmaids.*

EMILY ANN (*Calling*): I'm so excited! I'm so excited!
I just can't tell you!

REVERSE SHOT *looking across Emily Ann to the people down on the sidewalk.*

EMILY ANN (*Shouting down*): I want to thank you all
for the presents and all!

BRIDESMAID (*Calling back*): Call me up tomorrow and
let me know how you feel!

*Laughter from some of the wedding party and gig-
gles from the Negro children. The GI who has climbed
into one of the cars, says:*

THE BEST MAN: Can I give anybody a lift?

THE MOTHER: Goodbye, honey!

EMILY ANN: Goodbye, Ma, goodbye! See you Monday!

*The mother gets into the uncle's car, the last to get
in. The door closes behind her. The cars start off. Emily
Ann watches them disappear, then stands a moment,*

*pensive, a little troubled, then turns, opens the screen
door and goes into the apartment.*

INTERIOR. *The living room.* WIDE FULL SHOT *showing Emily Ann entering and Tower at the punch bowl
pouring himself a glass. He is dressed neatly in his olive
drabs, sober but distant, detached, isolated, inside himself. She regards him a little anxiously.*

EMILY ANN: I want to thank you very much for going
through with the ceremony, the formalities, the
minister and all that. I know how you despise little
formalities like that, but they are deeply important
to me, and I appreciate . . . *(She breaks off)*

*Tower merely nods, sips his punch, looks vaguely
around the shabby little room, all the more shabby for
the half-eaten wedding cake, the plates with portions of
cake left on them, the glasses and tumblers here and
there. He goes to the porch door, stands. There is a feeling of hostility in him.*

EMILY ANN: I expect I better clean up a little bit now.

*She gathers a few plates and starts for the kitchen.
Before she reaches the doorway, she pauses and looks at
her husband. He is examining his glass of punch. She is
anxiously aware of his coldness.*

EMILY ANN: Are you all right? Do you feel all right?

TOWER: I feel fine.

EMILY ANN: What are you thinking about?

TOWER: Nothing.

EMILY ANN: Give me a chance, Johnny.

TOWER (*Whirling to face her, his eyes blazing*): I said
I feel fine! Go clean up the dishes or whatever
you're doing!

*He turns angrily back to looking out through the
screen door, and the room is suddenly still, thick with
the hush of restrained hatred. After a moment, Emily
Ann moves a few steps into the room, afraid to look at
him.*

EMILY ANN: Don't turn your back on me. Give me a
chance.

TOWER: Just leave me alone right now, Emmy. That
would be the best thing for you to do.

*She doesn't move. She stands in the middle of the
room, afraid to let go of the fumbling moment of con-
tact she has made.*

TOWER: Leave me alone right now. Let me find my own
way. I'll try to make this work out. Just leave me
alone right now.

MEDIUM LONG SHOT *looking past the sad little half-eaten wedding cake, past Emily Ann standing in the middle of the room, her eyes closed, her shoulders slumped, her stomach taut, her heart cold, to Tower standing rigidly at the porch screen door staring stonily out into the night. And so they were married. Hold this tableau for a moment.*

DISSOLVE TO *Exterior. Street outside Emily Ann's home. Day.* GROUP SHOT *of four little Negro kids dressed in winter clothes, interrupted in their play, looking down the street.*

THEIR POV: *Looking down the shabby, unsidewalked street with its uneven row of old frame houses, some of them unpainted. It is not quite dusk; the sun is low in the west, and there is a heavy golden sheen in the air. What the little kids are fascinated by is Tower soddenly drunk, lurching down the street toward the house he now lives in. His Army greatcoat is unbuttoned and flaps limply as he staggers along. He passes the kids; they eye him covertly. He turns into the house and starts climbing up the stairs with the painfully meticulous caution of the very drunk.*

INTERIOR. *Emily Ann's apartment.* FULL SHOT *of Tower opening the door, then the screen door, then poising in the open doorway to make sure of his balance.*

REVERSE SHOT *of Emily Ann, eight months pregnant, full and swollen, crossing to the kitchen. We see enough of Tower's face to see the sodden distaste he has for this bulging, waddling girl. He shuffles across the gray, shadowed living room to the kitchen doorway. Still across his shoulder we see Emily Ann and her mother at work in the kitchen preparing the evening meal: the mother a frumpy woman of forty, in a torn house dress and flapping slippers, one stocking loose and hanging on one leg, singing softly her inevitable hymns, and the very pregnant girl, sallow and without make-up. The mother stands at the stove absently watching a saucepan of boiling water. Emily Ann is at the cupboard pouring her shelled peas into a saucepan. She places her hand on her swollen stomach as the baby kicks hard within her. Neither of them cares to acknowledge Tower's presence.*

TOWER: Well, I finally got myself transferred to a combat outfit. I leave a week from Tuesday. I hope I get killed.

Emily Ann looks at him, the cold hatred manifest in her eyes.

EMILY ANN: I hope so too.

She turns to an opened package of chopped meat and begins rolling the meat into patties. Tower turns after a moment, shuffles back across the living room and goes out the door.

Long shot *looking past the four Negro kids as they watch Tower lurching back into the street he had just come down. We watch him with the kids for a moment, till he is quite down the block.*

Dissolve to *Exterior. A street. Night.* Full shot *of Tower sitting on the curb of this quiet, dark residential street, staring with drunken blankness at the street. It is drizzling, and his face is moist, his greatcoat soggy wet. He closes his eyes and then slowly allows his weary, besotted body to slide into a reclining position. His knees curl up, and he lies, a grotesque, wet embryo of a man, half on the curb, half in the gutter, sleeping in the drizzle.*

Dissolve to *Interior. Emily Ann's apartment, living room.* Full shot *of Emily Ann lying on the floor of the living room reading movie magazines. They are all around her:* Modern Screen, Photoplay, *etc. She wears a skirt, sloppy-Joe sweater and saddle shoes and looks even younger than her eighteen years. She is no longer pregnant. The apartment is quiet. There are a few slight changes. On the walls hang portrait upon portrait of movie stars of that day, carefully scissored from the magazines—*Ann Sheridan, Cary Grant, Deanna Durbin, Ann Rutherford, Mickey Rooney, Gene Tierney, Pau-

lette Goddard, John Payne, Betty Grable, Errol Flynn, Victor Mature, etc. A baby cries faintly off in another room, and Emily Ann frowns, cocks her head, waits to hear if it will continue. The baby cries plaintively again, and Emily Ann gets to her feet with a small sign of exasperation. The baby now begins to cry fully. Emily Ann moves to the bedroom.

    INTERIOR. *The bedroom.* MEDIUM SHOT *looking across and through the bars of a crib to the door of the bedroom as Emily Ann enters. There is a very small baby, hardly the size of your forearm, lying under a thin receiving blanket, only its face showing, crying lustily. Emily Ann moves to the crib, a soft smile edging her lips. She murmurs soothing endearments as she approaches.*

EMILY ANN: All right, sweetie baby. All right, sweetie baby. Don't you worry now. Mommie's going to kiss you.

    She picks up the crying baby, receiving blanket and all, and presses it to her. Her eyes close and she hugs it in a flush of love for the child.

EMILY ANN: Sweet baby, sweet baby, sweet baby . . .

    The baby continues to cry. Emily Ann walks around with it.

EMILY ANN: What do you want, baby? What do you want? You just had your bottle. Baby, baby, baby, baby.

The shrill thin screams begin to get on Emily Ann's nerves. She frowns.

EMILY ANN (*Muttering, with no real vigor*): Shut up, shut up, shut up.

She goes out the bedroom, across the living room, into the kitchen. The baby's cry continues without pause, a disturbing, thin wail.

EMILY ANN: Come on, I'll give you the rest of the bottle. You want the rest of the bottle?

There is a half-filled baby bottle on the cupboard shelf. She picks it up. The baby's cry is becoming nerve-wracking.

EMILY ANN (*Frustrated, losing her patience*): What's the matter? What's the matter? (*She feels the baby's rump under the blanket*) Are you wet? What is it? (*The nerve-wracking little cry continues*) Do you want the bottle? Here. Do you want the bottle? (*The baby cries*) Shut up, shut up, shut up. (*Crying out*) What do you want? (*The angry voice only makes the baby cry louder. Emily Ann is on the verge of tears herself, screams out)* Shut up! Shut up! Leave me alone! Leave me alone!

She goes out of the kitchen, across the living room again, and walks aimlessly around the living room. She is crying now in desperation. The baby is crying with almost unbearable shrillness. Emily Ann moves up and down the bare living room, holding the screaming baby, crying.

EMILY ANN *(Whimpering):* Please . . . please . . . please . . .

She clenches her eyes against the baby's screaming and shuffles back to the bedroom.

EMILY ANN: Oh, my God, my God, my God!

She puts the baby back into the crib, where it lies squalling. It has now been crying in this piercing fashion for at least a minute. It is unbearable. Emily Ann sits down, stares aghast around the room, shaking her head nervously, crying. DISSOLVE TO *Interior. The kitchen.*

FULL SHOT *of Emily Ann standing by the window on the far wall, staring out with hostile bleakness. The sun is strong, and there is an edge of frost on the window. Together, these effects combine almost to whiten Emily Ann's face like an overexposed snapshot. She turns at the sound of the door being opened.*

MEDIUM WIDE SHOT *showing Emily Ann turning to the doorway through which her mother, bundled in a winter coat, is now entering. The mother, vaguely aware something is amiss, looks across to her daughter through steel-rimmed glasses.*

EMILY ANN: I'm getting out of here. I'm getting out of this town. I want to leave the baby with you, Ma. It's too much for me. I can't stand it no more!

THE MOTHER: What's the matter?

EMILY ANN *(Crying out):* I'm only eighteen years old! I got a good figure! I turn lots of heads when I go down the street. I want to have some fun!

THE MOTHER: What about the baby?

EMILY ANN *(Shrilly):* I don't want it! I don't want it! I didn't want it when it was born and I don't want her now!

TWO SHOT *shooting across the mother's face to Emily Ann by the window. The familiarity of Emily Ann's words bring an expression of deep pain to the mother's rock-ribbed face. The cycle is complete. Emily Ann stands by the window, her face bleached by the white glare of the snow outside and the fierce stream of sunlight, her chin quivering with a terrified desperation.*

EMILY ANN: I want to be happy!

FADE OUT.

FADE IN *on Exterior. Sunset Boulevard and Laurel Canyon. Hollywood. Day.*

MEDIUM LONG SHOT *looking down Sunset Boulevard in the direction of Highland Avenue. For orientation purposes, if we were to turn around we would see Schwab's drugstore and the parking lot where the old Actor's Lab used to be. Right now we see a row of gasoline stations in the background, a dry-cleaning store, a delicatessen, and some other stores. We also single out Rita Shawn, Hollywood starlet (nee Emily Ann Faulkner), walking toward us. She is twenty-one years old by now, a little too blond. The black dress is too tight around the hips; the high heels are too high. She seems brassier, bolder, less vulnerable. She carries a large flat portfolio, the sort artists' models carry to show their pictures. It is a bright, warm hazy Hollywood day. Over this, the following legend:*

PART TWO

Portrait of a Young Woman

CAMERA PANS *with Rita as she walks indolently toward us and then past us. Her dress buttons high on the neck and is demurely topped by a Peter Pan collar, but the hips undulate more than necessary and her breasts are straining against the material. The dress, frankly, was bought at Jack's on Wilshire, and it is a carefully selected size too small. Her blond hair falls in determinedly casual waves over her shoulders, and her lips glisten and sparkle. We watch her undulate away from us toward the Ham and Eggery on the corner of Laurel Canyon Drive. By the time she turns into the Ham and Eggery, we all know that this is a Hollywood starlet. Over this, the following legend:*

HOLLYWOOD, CALIFORNIA—
1947

INTERIOR. *The Ham and Eggery.* LONG SHOT *looking across the restaurant to the front door as Rita enters. This is one of those waffle joints that flourished briefly in Hollywood right after the war. The overhead ceiling fixture is in the shape of a huge skillet, and the eggs are served in a hot frying pan right off the fire. There are five rows of booths and a counter that runs up the length of one side. At the end of the counter there is an alcove that leads into the sudden darkness of a bar. The bar to this day is called the Black Watch. It is lunchtime and the place is crowded. All the patrons are actors, writers, or in some way connected with the movies. They are dressed after the casual fashion of Hollywood. The men wear sports shirts and slacks: the women wear men's shirts and slacks. There are a few dirndls and a few sports jackets. There is a noticeable sprinkling of sweat shirts and jeans, indicating that members of the Actor's Lab, a very serious school of acting, also patronize the place. There is a great deal of talking going on. The talk is angry, bitter, hostile and loud. Most of these people are regularly unemployed. Even the jokes are rancorous, the laughter harsh.*

MEDIUM SHOT *showing Rita making her way down an aisle toward a rear booth. In the foreground of the shot is a booth occupied by three young men and two young actresses. This is a contingent of the sweat-shirt brigade, and the discussions at tables like this stem from two major issues—the commercial mediocrity of Hollywood and the paranoid insistence that the whole society is preventing these chaps from getting their big break. The chap holding forth at the moment is a writer who writes one-act plays of studied social content crackling with violent pungencies of dialogue. Actually, he talks a great deal more than he writes. He is talking now.*

69

THE WRITER: Name one good picture made in the United States in the last five years! Go ahead! Name one. I mean a good picture! Have we had one *Open City*? One *Shoeshine*? We don't have a director in this country to compare to Rossellini! De Sica! How can you compare American pictures to foreign pictures?

AN ACTOR: How about *Oxbow Incident*?

THE WRITER: All right. One good picture. All right. Name another.

ANOTHER ACTOR: *Lost Weekend*.

THE WRITER: All right. Two good pictures.

FIRST ACTOR: *Grapes of Wrath*.

THE WRITER: All right. Three good pictures. (*He is losing interest in the argument*)

FULL SHOT *of Rita approaching a rear-wall table at which sit two other starlets, one blonde and one brunette. The blonde's name is Hillary and the brunette's name is Joanna. They are both dressed in blouses and slacks. The blonde is a vapid type with undistinguished features. The brunette is an enormously sad girl. She stares down at a shot of liquor with naked distaste for the liquor and all of life itself. She appears to have had a bad night the night before, a night of strange dreams; some of the horror is still with her. Both girls are in their late twenties. They look up briefly as Rita approaches. There is a muttered exchange of hellos.*

RITA: Where is everybody?

JOANNA *(Scowling darkly at her drink):* Dutch Seymour called you about ten minutes after you left the house.

RITA *(Amiably):* I better call him.

HILLARY *(Offering a copy of a newspaper to Rita):* You're in Ed Sullivan's column again today.

RITA *(Sitting at the table):* Yeah, I know. *(To Joanna)* Was Dutch mad?

JOANNA *(Not looking up):* My mother answered the phone.

HILLARY *(Pointing to the paper):* Where it says "Boxing champ Dutch Seymour is talking wedding bells to starlet Rita Shawn, who used to be Emily Ann Faulkner of Beacon City, Maryland." What did he put all that in for?

RITA *(Brightly):* Oh, I called Joe Glass yesterday. I said, "Joe, Dutch Seymour has been asking me to marry him. Is that worth an item somewhere?" So I said, "Joe, if you get it into some column," I said, "ask them to put my real name down. Because my mother—I called her last week—she says nobody back in Beacon City believes all the clippings I sent back is really me. It always says starlet Rita Shawn." So I said, "Put down that my real name was Emily Ann Faulkner." My mama didn't even know who Dutch was. I said, "Ma, Dutch Seymour is an all-time boxing great. He was middleweight

champ, retired undefeated and beat Slapsie Maxie
Rosenbloom for the light heavyweight crown, fighting out of his own weight class." So my mama said,
"Slapsie Maxie who, precious?" *(To Joanna, who
stands now and starts off for the bar)* How do you
feel, Joanna, after last night?

*Joanna doesn't seem to have heard. She pads off
into the blackness of the bar. Rita regards the empty
glass on the table.*

RITA: Well, she's drinking before lunch now, I see.
HILLARY: Oh, she's had about five shots already.

*Rita has spotted somebody up in front of the restau-
rant and is gaily waving at him.*

RITA *(Broad smile, gay):* Hiya, Alex! *(Turns to Hillary,
the smile disappearing. She darts a quick look at
the bar)* You should have seen Joanna last night.
She's been drinking something terrible. It's just
breaking her mother's heart. I'm going to move out
of there. There's just nothing but screaming going
on in that house all the time. Who you rooming
with now, Hillary?
HILLARY: I'm rooming with Sandra Steele.
RITA: Oh, I thought she was rooming with Sharlene.
HILLARY: They had a fight.

RITA (*Intense whisper*): I came home last night. I was out with Martin Charles, who's doing an independent with all unknowns. There's a nice little part in that picture, four days' work at least, a Nazi girl who hides out the aviator on her father's farm when he's running away from the Storm Troopers. Anyway, Martin Charles took me to my door. He's got big eyes for me. I think I'll get that part. Anyway, I came in the house. It was two A.M. Joanna was sitting in the living room with all the shades up, wearing just about nothing, talking to herself. She was so drunk, she didn't know I was there. She made me think of my first husband. Did I tell you my final divorce papers came through?

HILLARY: Does Dutch Seymour really want to marry you?

RITA (*She suddenly beams and waves brightly to somebody off stage*): I don't know what he sees in me. I only been in seven pictures, and only two of those was speaking parts. I must say, however, that ever since that item appeared in Ed Sullivan's this morning, I got four calls. I just come back from Hal King at Metro. I'm going up to see Burt Harres at Paramount in about forty minutes. His secretary called this morning.

HILLARY: Well, if you're going up to see Burt Harres, I wouldn't wear anything so high in the neck.

RITA: I just thought I'd try something demure for a change.

HILLARY: I know a couple of girls been out with Dutch Seymour, and they say he's pretty dull.

RITA: Oh, he's been out with about every girl in Hollywood. He's a lost soul. He really is. It's hard for a man to be a big athletic celebrity for so many years and then retire and be nothing. He don't know what to do with himself. He wanders around the country making speeches to Boy Scouts. He sits there in that hotel room of his, calling his friends on the telephone all day long. He calls me twice a day. I thought about marrying him, because it would be wonderful for my career. *(She stands)* I better call Dutch. *(She suddenly spots another familiar face off stage and waves and beams)* Watch my portfolio, will you, Hillary? *(She moves off into the bar)*

INTERIOR. *The bar.* FULL SHOT *of Rita coming into the bar, erect and undulating, the professional half-formed smile nailed on her face. The bar is dark, with only a few little hidden lights by the bar mirror. There are about three people in it, the bar having just opened. At the end of the bar by the telephone booths is Joanna, standing hunched over her drink. She watches Rita as she comes to the phone booth.*

JOANNA *(A girl who can drink for hours without showing it):* Where are you going this afternoon?

RITA *(Sliding into the phone booth and fishing change*

out of her purse): Well, I'm up for a part at Burt
   Harres' at Columbia at two-thirty.
JOANNA: I'll drive over with you.
RITA *(Inserting a dime and dialing):* Fine, if you want
   to, Joanna. *(She finishes dialing, waits)*
JOANNA: There's a letter from your husband.
RITA: Yes, I saw it. *(On phone)* Room 417, please. Mr.
   Dutch Seymour. *(To Joanna)* Usual letter. He's fine.
   My little daughter's fine. He's working in a publishing house now. He's getting married again. He's
   being psychoanalyzed. *(On phone)* Hiya, Dutch?
   Dutch, this is Rita. . . . Well, I just . . . Dutch,
   I don't know who put that item in Ed Sullivan's. I
   didn't tell anybody, not even Joanna and her
   mother. *(She makes a moue at Joanna, rolls her eyes
   at the ceiling, sighs with impatience)* Well, maybe
   you told somebody, and it was overheard. You
   know how you can't say a word around this town
   without it getting in the papers.

DISSOLVE TO *Exterior. Studio street, Columbia stu-
dios.* TWO SHOT *of Rita and Joanna sitting in a Ford
convertible. The car is parked at the curb. The blank
white stucco sound stages and studio buildings rise
monolithically and blankly all around them. There is a
desultory pedestrian traffic, a person here and there
shuffling across the hot sunny streets. The girls are both
sitting silently, disturbed, depressed.*

75

RITA *(After a moment)*: You need any money?

JOANNA: No, my mother's alimony came in yesterday. I swiped twenty bucks.

RITA: I got about a hundred dollars you can have if you want it. What's eating you, Joanna? You been going on like this for ever so long.

JOANNA: Don't you ever get depressed?

RITA: Sure.

JOANNA *(With growing surliness)*: When I first met you, you were about one step away from picking men off the street. You were going to throw yourself off the top of the May Building. You don't remember that, do you? You just got fired, and you didn't have any money, and you kept talking about going up to the personnel manager's office and throwing yourself out of the window. That's how you were going to show him for firing you. Well, that's how I feel. I feel so tired I can hardly get out of bed in the morning. The only reason I get up at all is I just couldn't stand staying home with my mother. You better get upstairs. You're going to be late for Burt Harres.

RITA: I got ten minutes.

JOANNA: Well, just don't tell me to stop drinking all the time.

She stares sullenly out at the glaring bright white stucco of the studio buildings. Rita sits uncomfortably.

JOANNA *(Abruptly):* When I was eight years old, I won
the Prettiest Child at the Missouri State County
Fair, and that's all my mother had to hear. She
whisked me up to New York, and she had me taking ballet lessons at Carnegie Hall. Whole bunch
of us little girls prancing around on our skinny legs.
She had me modeling for John Robert Powers
when I was fifteen years old. I made eleven thousand dollars when I was fifteen years old. Well, I
been out here eleven years now, and it's about time
she realizes she ain't never going to be the mother
of a big movie star. If you don't make it by the time
you're twenty-eight, you never make it. I'm taking
extra calls now, standing on line, making eyes at
some assistant director. I don't know how to get out
of this, don't you understand? I don't know where
to go. I keep dreaming I'll meet some man who will
marry me and take me away. Who, Eddie Rogers?
I been going with him for four months, and I don't
even like him. He's a vicious drunk; I never know
what he's going to do. And after him somebody just
like him. I wish I could just go to sleep and sleep
and sleep.

RITA: You want to go to the beach this afternoon? I
think Valerie and Marilyn went there.

JOANNA: It's two-thirty now.

*They sit in stiff silence again. After a moment,
Joanna darts a quick look at her young friend.*

JOANNA: I really do believe you are concerned about me.

RITA: I am, Joanna.

JOANNA: You'd really give me that hundred dollars, wouldn't you? Where would you get a hundred dollars anyway? Dutch Seymour give you money? Why don't you marry him? Don't you like him at all?

RITA: Sure, I like him. I like him a lot. He's a kind man. I just don't want to get involved, that's all.

JOANNA: I'd marry him in a minute.

RITA: Joanna, I never had it so good as right now. I got a lot of friends, and I go to a lot of parties, and I got nice clothes. My mother writes me I'm the hero of my home town. Everybody is following my career like I was a football player from the high school who went on to Notre Dame. We had a boy like that. My, how we all talked about him. What do I want to get married for? I'm having a fine time just the way I am.

JOANNA: It's better than drinking yourself to sleep.

RITA: Well, the day I find myself with nothing else to do but drink myself to sleep, I'll get married. I never drank in my life. I can't stand the taste of it. I saw what my first husband was like, and I won't even sip a cocktail at a party.

JOANNA: Well, I hope you never have to start.

RITA: I never will, don't you worry.

JOANNA: Don't be mad at me, Rita.

*A sudden swift compassion sweeps over Rita's
angry little face. She leans toward her friend in a flush
of warmth.*

RITA *(Sincerely):* I ain't mad at you, Joanna. You're the
only person I know I feel something for, and it
makes me sick to see you as miserable as you are.

JOANNA *(Touched):* You better get up to see Burt
Harres.

RITA *(Peering at her friend):* Joanna . . .

JOANNA: Could you lend me ten bucks, something like
that?

RITA *(Promptly opening her purse):* Sure.

*A portly, middle-aged man comes out of the build-
ing behind the car, preoccupied, starts walking down
the street. His appearance transforms the dejected
Joanna into a brightly smiling young woman, her mouth
somewhat ajar in the now common conception of sensuality.*

JOANNA *(Brightly):* Hiya, Mr. Cummings!

*Rita looks up, her face automatically registering a
vivid, flashing smile.*

RITA: Hiya, Mr. Cummings!

Mr. Cummings turns, nods, and continues on his

*way. Camera stays on the two young starlets, their faces
a study in facile gaiety.*

DISSOLVE TO *Interior. Burt Harres' outer office.*
WIDE SHOT *showing Rita and four other girls, all blond,
all cut from the same cloth, almost indistinguishable
from each other, perched and sitting on the long brown
leather office couch or on the comfortable soft brown
leather easy chair or standing against the wall. All the
girls are dressed fit to kill according to their own lights.
For the most part, this consists of daring necklines and
much too tight skirts. They all have large artists' models'
portfolios or smaller books of pictures of themselves.
They all sit with a determined jadedness, unmoving,
their skirts arranged over their knees. A gray-haired secretary sits behind the desk, drinking coffee from a container and mumbling indistinct words to a friend over
the telephone. There are some prints on the wall, Japa-
nese silks and hunting scenes, and a framed poster of
Mr. Harres' last picture, an effort entitled* Give Me My
Blood. *Next to the poster is a mounted bronze plaque
which is a box-office award for the aforementioned picture distributed by one of the innumerable organiza-
tions that bestow box-office awards. The door to the inner office opens, and still another pretty blond girl comes
out, expressionless except for a thin little smile. She
looks at one of her friends sitting on the couch and
makes a small moue to indicate something every one of
these girls understands. The girl she made the face at,*

*sitting two away from Rita, offers the girl who just came
out a cigarette. She mutters:*

THE GIRL WHO JUST CAME OUT: It ain't worth it. The
part's about that big.

*She indicates how big the part is by her thumb and
forefinger held one inch apart. Rita stands, goes to the
secretary's desk.*

RITA *(To the secretary)*: Rita Shawn.
SECRETARY: All right, honey.

*She goes to the door to the inner office, raps lightly,
opens it, sticks her head in.*

INTERIOR. *Burt Harres' office.* MEDIUM LONG SHOT
*looking across Burt Harres' bulky back to the doorway
where Rita stands, peering in with a big smile.*

RITA: Can I come in?
HARRES: Come on in.

*Rita comes in, closes the door. Mr. Harres' office is
precisely the same as his secretary's except that there is
an air conditioner that clogs up his window. The window has white nylon curtains through which the Hollywood sun filters. There is a picture of Mr. Harres' wife
and two children, aged sixteen and nine, on Mr. Harres'*

desk. Mr. Harres himself is a tall, well-groomed, bald-ing man in his fifties, dressed in impeccable business costume, a gray striped suit. He looks up briefly at Rita's entrance and then goes back to pacing the room with executive ponderousness. He keeps his right hand in his jacket pocket and talks in measured basso tones. There are several scripts on the desk, variously colored, and a small vase containing innumerable finely sharpened pencils. Rita advances with her portfolio.

RITA: I have my pictures with me, if you'd like to see them, Mr. Harres. I had a very nice part in my last picture at Columbia. Michael Sillman directed. *The Wayward Angel.* I play a sweet sort of South-ern girl type. I think—

HARRES: I got a small part in my picture. A barmaid in a Western town. I've had my eye on you for some time, Miss . . . *(He looks quickly at a sheet of paper on his desk)* Miss Shawn. You'd be just right for it. You be nice to me, and I'll see that you get billing. It'll be a good credit for you.

RITA *(The smile gone from her face, all business):* How nice do I have to be?

HARRES *(His face suddenly brightens into a smile):* You're Dutch Seymour's girl. That's right. Sure. You'll get the part. We'll talk about it tonight. Rita Shawn. Sure.

RITA *(Smiling):* Are you going to pick me up or do I have to meet you somewheres?

HARRES: Why don't you meet me at the Ready Room. Seven o'clock.

Rita nods, gathers up her portfolio, and reaches for the doorknob.

DISSOLVE TO *Exterior. Hollywood. Night.* HIGH ANGLE SHOT *looking down the hill of North Cherokee, showing Hollywood at night, a small six-story apartment house in foreground. There are some lights on.*

INTERIOR. *Living room of an apartment.* MEDIUM LONG SHOT *of Burt Harres moving slowly, restlessly around the room. He is wearing a dressing gown over his clothes. His face is expressionless, perhaps even cold. He seems unpleasantly preoccupied. His right hand is stiffly placed in the pocket of the robe. Two standing lamps illumine the room. Through the Venetian blinds we can see that it is night outside. The room itself is furnished after the usual style of studio apartments, several day beds, soft chairs, an Eames chair, a portable bar with bottles of liquor and a variety of glasses, wallpaper showing small sporting scenes, a pipe rack running almost the length of the wall. Burt Harres moves slowly around the room, right hand in pocket, the perpetual executive pacing his conference.*

The door to another room opens, and Rita comes out. She is wearing a party dress. She seems calm, de-

tached, a cigarette dangling listlessly from her lips. Neither of the two people looks at the other.

HARRES *(Coldly):* I called a cab for you. Wait downstairs for it.

RITA *(Squeezing her feet into her pumps, all business):* I told my agent I had the part. He'll call you in the morning, discuss terms.

HARRES: Hundred dollars a day. Two days' shooting. There's nothing to discuss.

RITA: When's my shooting date? *(Picking up a script from off a studio couch)* Is this the script? I'll take it home and study the part. I'll tell my agent to call you in the morning.

Rita picks her summer stole off the back of one of the chairs, and her tiny beaded purse.

RITA *(Smiling amiably):* Well, thank you for a very pleasant evening. I enjoyed the dinner very much. Is this my cab money? *(She smiles pleasantly, scoops up a bill from off the coffee table)* Goodbye now.

Harres says nothing, is slowly pacing the room. Rita fits her stole over her shoulders and disappears into the shadows of the front corridor.

DISSOLVE TO *Exterior. Street outside this apartment*

house. Night. LONG SHOT *looking down the hill of North Cherokee with Rita in foreground. She stands, her arms folded across her chest, pulling the stole tight across her shoulders. Looking past her, we can see all the way to Sunset Boulevard. It is eleven o'clock at night, and the endless swishing parade of automobile lights moves back and forth on the boulevards. Some of the store fronts in the distance are still lighted, and neons blink in the dark night. A taxicab has rounded the corner at the bottom of the hill and drives quickly up to where she stands in front of the small white apartment house.*

CLOSE SHOT *of Rita getting into the cab. She sits down and then just sits for a moment. The driver finally turns around.*

DRIVER: Where to?
RITA: I don't know.

She stares listlessly at the floor of the cab.

DISSOLVE TO *Interior. The Ham and Eggery.* WIDE GROUP SHOT *of a booth containing three young actors and two girls. One of the girls is Rita; she seems quite tired. She rests her face on her right hand and rubs the corners of her eyes. In the background we see that the restaurant is jumping, filled with people, loud voices, loud laughs. One of the three men in the booth is the writer of the previous Ham and Eggery scene. Some of this restau-*

rant's patrons never leave the joint, smoking, drinking coffee, and talking all day long right up to closing time at 1:00 A.M. The writer is one of these fellows. He is in full blast of discussion as we cut in.

THE WRITER: Acting! You call that acting? A smile— that's joy? A frown—that's tragedy?

The other girl in the booth, an intense little brunette with a mop of hair and disdainfully dressed in a sweat shirt and dungarees, leans toward Rita.

THE GIRL: You want a Dexedrine Spansule?
RITA: Yeah, you got one?

The girl fishes a little tin out of her pocket and gives Rita a Spansule, which she gulps down with her coffee. She sits slumped in her seat, her face resting heavily on the palm of her hand. Camera begins to dolly slowly back and away from the booth. The writer's words begin to fade into the over-all jumble of the restaurant just as this particular booth begins to get lost among all the other booths.

THE WRITER: All right, wise guy. Name me one good picture made in the United States in the last five years. Name me one picture to compare with *Open City* or *Shoeshine*. Name me one picture that's got guts. Right now, I'm writing a play that exposes this stinking industry for what it is.

ACTOR: When do you write, George? You're here gassing away all day and night.

LONG SHOT *looking down on the restaurant, only half filled with tired and driven people. In particular, we see Rita hunched in her seat, exhausted and spent, her face too weary to feign any cheerfulness.*

DISSOLVE TO *Interior. The bar.* FULL SHOT *of Rita in the dark bar, which is jammed. Actors, actresses—old, young, middle-aged—assistant directors, writers, grips, gaffers, and prop men block the aisle and make it almost impassable. Rita has joined a huddled group at the end of the bar. There are two starlets sitting on stools sipping drinks, surrounded by four men. Rita is beaming, hyper-ebullient, hysterically gay. She wraps her arms around two of the men in a burst of effusive camaraderie. Somebody offers her a drink. She says, "No, thanks. I don't drink." Her face is radiant, almost hysterically so. The two starlets on the stools say something. Rita bends down to hear it, then throws her head back and laughs and laughs and laughs.*

DISSOLVE TO *Exterior. North Sierra Bonita. Night.* HIGH ANGLE SHOT *looking down on the dark, deserted, silent little street of pretty little one-family houses. For a long moment, the absolute stillness hangs so that we know it is very late at night. Not a light in any window. All is quiet. Then a taxi edges slowly into our view, moving along at the curb, looking for a particular house. The taxi stops. The door opens and Rita gets out of the cab, closes the door behind her. The click of the door is clearly audible in the night hush. The cab pulls away with a murmur of gears and motor.*

FULL SHOT *of Rita hurrying up the little white walk to the front door of the house, fishing out her key from her purse. She inserts the key and opens the door. We can perhaps detect through the white chintz curtains that a lamp is on deep in the living room.*

INTERIOR. *Rita's home.* FULL SHOT *of Rita coming into the house, closing the door behind her. She turns; the house is quiet, but the vague indication of light makes her turn from the small entrance foyer and take a few steps into the living room.*

RITA'S POV: *The living room is dark except for one small reading lamp at the far end. Its thin light throws a vague illumination over the modest room, which is half dining and half living room. The furniture is Victorian, uncomfortable-looking chairs on spindly legs and an uncomfortable couch. A small mahogany dining table is surrounded by small mahogany dining chairs. Sprawled in one of the soft chairs is Joanna, soddenly, heavily drunk. Her shoes are off and lie on their sides in front of her. One of her stockings makes a wispy bundle on the shadowy floor. Her blouse is unbuttoned and hangs loosely outside of her slacks. On the floor lies a bottle of gin on its side, half of it spilled onto the rug in an ugly blotch. There is also an ice-cube container from the refrigerator on the floor, and beside Joanna's chair is a highball glass containing one ice cube. She regards Rita's entrance through swollen, heavy-lidded eyes. Her face is sullen and thick with drunken pain. The light of the lamp falls fitfully on her features, shadowing and distorting them.*

REACTION SHOT OF RITA. Expressionless. FULL SHOT of Rita standing watching her friend. Then she sidles slowly across the room toward Joanna, who is now look-ing down at the floor. Rita sinks onto the couch, which forms an el to the chair Joanna sits in. For a moment she just sits there. Then she bends down, picks up the gin bottle and pours some into the highball glass on the end table. Then she takes the glass and begins to sip it. Her face remains expressionless throughout all this. Now she kicks off her shoes, leans back and stretches her feet out in front of her. Her eyes close. She sips the drink.

LONG SHOT looking down the length of the living room to the two starlets sprawled on their seats, the small disarray of a small drunken binge on the carpet in front of them. Not a word is said for a long moment.

89

Then Rita stands, holding her drink, sipping it as she walks down the living room toward the telephone sitting on the coffee table directly in front of camera. She sits down in the chair beside the phone, lifts the receiver, sets it down on the coffee table, dials, sipping her gin throughout. She picks up the receiver, holds it to her ear, looks vaguely, even with boredom, around the room.

RITA *(On phone):* Room 417, please. Mr. Dutch Seymour. *(She waits, making short sighs of frustration and tenseness, and then suddenly downs the rest of her drink in one gulp. The taste is forbidding and she clenches her eyes against it. Then, with her eyes still closed, she says):* Well, hello, Dutch. This is Rita. I hope I didn't wake you up. I know how you stay up late reading all the time. . . . No, I just got in. . . . Well, I tell you, Dutch . . . *(She looks up at the ceiling, bored, tired)* I feel like getting married. Do you still want to marry me, Dutch? Yeah, sure, any time. I promise you I'll make you a very good wife. Dutch . . .

DISSOLVE TO *Exterior. Grauman's Chinese Theater. Night.*

MEDIUM LONG SHOT *of Rita and Dutch sweeping up to the entrance of the theater. This is a première, and there are a number of excitable spectators flanking the entrance walk. Rita beams at them, waves, clutches her husband's arm. He is a tall, somber, well-built, light-haired man of thirty-eight. He smiles at his wife's child-like excitement.*

DISSOLVE TO *Interior. Grauman's Chinese Theater.* FULL SHOT *of Rita and Dutch seated off the aisle. A small bespectacled man is bent over them.*

CLOSE SHOT *of Rita being interviewed by the small bespectacled man.*

RITA: I never been so happy in all my life! We had a wonderful time in Acapulco on our honeymoon! I am absolutely deliriously happy.

INTERVIEWER: Do you believe marriage will interfere with your career?

RITA: Dutch and I think we are two intelligent people, and we see no reason why I can't have a career and be a wife too.

She darts a quick, nervous glance at her husband at her side. He is listening silently to a man at his side. Rita turns back to the interviewer with a patient, waiting smile.

DISSOLVE TO *Exterior. Beverly Hills Hotel. Day.* LONG ESTABLISHING SHOT *of the hotel entrance, considerable activity, cars pulling in and out, people waiting to be picked up.*

INTERIOR. *Beverly Hills Hotel lobby. Day.* MEDIUM LONG SHOT *showing the crowded lobby.* CLOSE SHOT *of switchboard with crowded lobby in background.*

SWITCHBOARD OPERATOR: Mr. Seymour isn't taking any calls yet.

INTERIOR. *Rita's and Dutch's suite at hotel.* MEDIUM LONG SHOT *noting Rita and Dutch asleep on their respective twin beds. The Venetian blinds are drawn tightly and the room seems dark and close. The sun, as we have seen in previous shots, is very strong today, and the close air of the bedroom seems muggy. Rita sleeps with only a sheet covering her. Dutch has a light blanket over him, one bare, hairy arm visible over it. One of the bedspreads has been piled loosely on a soft chair; the other lies in a heap on the floor at the foot of the bed. Clothes seem to have been left at random here and there—a shirt, Rita's stockings, Dutch's shoes, a woman's white silk blouse. The total effect is one of heat and disorder and discomfort.*

CLOSER SHOT *of Rita waking up with Dutch sleeping in background. She wakes up conscious of the closeness of the air, her eyes red, not fully rested. She lies quietly for a moment, conscious of an unpleasant taste in her mouth and a sad, amorphous weight in her stomach. She sits up after a moment and lets her legs dangle over the side of her bed. She faces her husband's bed and watches him expressionlessly for a moment. She wears limp, blue pajamas, clinging in small patches to her wet skin. She picks up the house phone, waits a moment.*

RITA *(Low murmur):* What time is it? . . . As late as that? Think I can still get some breakfast out of room service? . . . No, I'll call later.

She hangs up and stands, stiff and yet not aching, with more of a feeling of desolation rather than physical discomfort. She pads on her bare feet across the green carpeting to the windows, opens one blind, reaches out and opens the window. This effort exhausts her, and she stands limply, frowning, catching her breath. The sudden sunlight streaming in through the one blind bleaches her face. She looks out over the palmetto and yucca trees to the busy, chattering activity at the car entrance to the hotel. Her face reveals a sad distaste for herself, the cluttered hotel room, the busy, bright sunlight. Behind her, her husband's voice reaches into the murky, slow movement of her thoughts.

DUTCH *(Muttering):* What time is it?

She turns. REVERSE SHOT *across her shoulder. Her husband lies silently on the bed. He has thrown back his covers, revealing a strong, brown, hirsute chest. He, too, seems drained.*

RITA: Half past one.

DUTCH: Boy, it's hot.

She moves silently back to her bed, sits down facing her husband, looks down at a copy of Look *magazine on the floor by her bare feet.*

RITA: I feel blue. I hate waking up with half the day gone already.

DUTCH: We ought to get up eight o'clock in the morning.

RITA: What'll we do eight o'clock in the morning?

DUTCH: I don't know. Go to the beach.

RITA: I'm sick of going to the beach. (*Rubs her temples. A dense, close silence fills the room*) You know how I feel? When I first came out here, I didn't know anybody. I used to stay up till two, three, four o'clock in the morning reading magazines. I wrote a letter to my father-in-law, care of the studio, but he never answered me. I used to sleep till one, two o'clock in the afternoon every day. I used to wake up sick in my heart. It's funny. I haven't thought about that in years. I hate waking up this late. I feel real blue. I really do. (*She lies back on her bed, stares up at the ceiling*) You ever feel that way, Dutch?

DUTCH: Sure.

RITA: You know what I used to do when I first came out here? I used to go into bars and let men think they could pick me up. Just to talk to somebody. I never drank in those days. I just used to sit with these guys till they got drunk and then I'd go home and read. Sometimes I'd fall asleep sitting up reading. I had a little room with an old Greek couple on South Orange Drive. I was so lonely I used to have the shakes like I had Parkinson's disease. But I never went home with any of those men. I just couldn't stand the thought of somebody touching me. I came close to going crazy in those days.

DUTCH *(Likewise lying on his bed staring up at the ceiling)*: You know, before we got married, I started to go to pieces myself. I used to take awful good care of myself. Every morning a shower and a shave. I couldn't stand it if my shoes weren't shiny. My people are St. Louis German, you know. We're awful clean. But the last half year or so I began going to pieces. Sometimes I wouldn't leave my hotel room for two days. I wouldn't shave. I used to look at the toothpaste. I couldn't stand the idea of the taste.

RITA: Why's that, Dutch?

DUTCH: Well, you know. Doing nothing all day, it eats up a man. That's no life. I don't know what I want to do, but I want to do something. Get into some business. You can be a retired sports star just so long. What do you think I ought to do?

RITA: I don't know. I'd like to get out of Hollywood, though.

Dutch gets up on one elbow.

DUTCH: Would you, really?
RITA: I'm not getting anywheres here, Dutch. I mean, why kid myself?

He examines her as she lies on her bed, a troubled blond girl in rumpled blue pajamas, her eyes closed now against the warmth of the room. After a moment, he lies back, staring at the ceiling. After another moment, he says:

DUTCH: Would you like to go back to St. Louis with me?

She turns her head on her pillow so that she can see him.

RITA: What would we do there, Dutch?
DUTCH (*Afraid to look at her, he stares at the ceiling*): Well, my father died. My brother's running the contracting business. They're doing very nicely. He's always writing me, my brother, to come back, get in the business. As a kid, I always liked hanging around my father, the cement and the mortar and the big trucks full of steel rods. I'd like to go back, I think, get into the business. I'm pretty important in St. Louis. People like me there. We'll get a nice house, have people to dinner. My mother's kind of

nosy, but if she gives you any trouble, just tell me. I'll straighten her out. You met my brother at the wedding. He liked you very much. I think that would be nice. It's real, you know, instead of floating around in mid-air like we are now.

He looks over to his wife and is a little startled to see that her eyes are filled with tears. He sits up, moves over to her bed, looks down at her with concerned tenderness.

DUTCH: It'll be nice, Rita. You'll like it.

She is suddenly in his arms, clutching at him, pressing her tear-streaked face against his chest.

RITA: Oh, Dutch, do you love me?
DUTCH: Sure.
RITA: Do you love me, Dutch?
DUTCH *(Holding her)*: I love you, Rita.
RITA: Let's do that, Dutch! Let's go to St. Louis. I got kin in St. Louis. I never met them.

He is holding her tightly, kissing her neck, her shoulders. She holds to him almost desperately, asking over and over again, "Do you love me, Dutch? Do you love me? Do you love me, Dutch?"

DISSOLVE TO *Interior. Their suite. Dusk.* MEDIUM LONG SHOT *looking across Rita lying in bed, showing most of the room. It is still in a state of disorder. It is dusk. A small breeze gently wafts the draperies; the windows are opened. Rita lies in bed, her bare shoulders and arms over the light blanket. A glass ash tray balances precariously on her stomach; she smokes a cigarette. She watches her husband as he moves across the room, a strong lithe man in pajama trousers. He goes into the bathroom, comes out again. She watches his every move with a growing sense of apprehension. He looks into his chest of drawers for underwear and socks. He is also smoking a cigarette.*

RITA *(Abruptly):* What do you mean you love me, Dutch?

He looks at her briefly.

RITA: What did I ever do for you? You know hundreds of girls. Why me? I'm not especially pretty. Why should anybody love me? I don't think very much of myself. If I was a man, I couldn't love me. In many ways, I'm a terrible girl. I have a three-year-old daughter, and I just gave her away to my first husband without even arguing. He sent me a paper in the mail, and I signed her entire custody away without even reading what the paper said. I never went to New York to visit her. I keep her out of my mind, I'm so ashamed of myself. I think I'm ugly. I'm dirty. I don't understand why you love me. I don't believe you. I don't think you love me. I think you're physically attracted to me. I don't even know why that. Why'd you marry me, Dutch? I came over any time you called me anyhow.

DUTCH *(Moving back across the room to the bathroom, carrying shorts and socks; amiably)*: I don't know what you're talking about.

He goes into the bathroom. Rita regards the opened doorway for a while.

RITA: What's it like when you love somebody, Dutch?

DUTCH *(Off screen in bathroom)*: Ain't you ever loved anybody?

RITA: Nobody ever loved me before. Why should you love me?

Dutch appears in the bathroom doorway. He is wearing a silk polka-dotted robe. His bare legs protrude below it.

DUTCH: You always try to act so tough, but you're like a little kid. That's the truth. I always liked little kids. My brother's kids, I'm crazy about them. I'm going to take a shower. We'll have dinner downstairs, then we're supposed to go to Burt Lancaster's.

He disappears back into the bathroom. Rita leans on one elbow, holding the sheet against her, regards the door to the bathroom.

RITA: I don't know what love is, Dutch. I find you very physically attractive, and I guess you find me very physically attractive, but that ain't going to last very long, Dutch.

The rush of the shower interrupts her. She calls once again:

RITA: Dutch . . .

He obviously doesn't hear her; she sinks back onto the bed, her pretty little face twisted into a thoughtful, anxious frown. She reaches around for the ash tray now at her side, drops a long ash into it.

DISSOLVE TO *Interior. Polo lounge, Beverly Hills Hotel.* TWO SHOT *of Rita and Dutch at dinner, with rest of restaurant in background. Their dinner is about over; they are on their coffee and dessert. A tall man in a sports jacket is bending over Dutch, talking inaudibly to him. Dutch is listening with a thin smile. Rita sits, her feeling of apprehension deepened on her face to the point of being obviously disturbed. Behind them, the dinner hour is in full progress, jangle and jammer. Dutch notes his wife's distracted mood.*

DUTCH: Something wrong, honey?

She smiles nervously, shakes her head, but the dark mood promptly returns to her face. The man talking to Dutch goes. Dutch looks at his wife again, purses his lips, wonders what's up.

RITA *(Suddenly):* Let's go upstairs again, Dutch.
DUTCH: Don't you want to go to Lancaster's?
RITA *(Standing and starting away):* Let's go upstairs.

DISSOLVE TO *Interior. Their suite.* FULL SHOT *of Rita in tears, in panic. Dutch listens to her with the patient fondness of a father. Through the window we can see it is night outside. The lamps in the room are lit.*

RITA *(In tears):* I don't want to go to St. Louis, Dutch!
DUTCH *(Consolingly):* All right, honey, we won't go.
RITA: You'll get tired of me.
DUTCH: What are you talking about?

He moves to her, tries to hold her, but she moves away from him in panic.

RITA: You'll leave me, you'll desert me. What would you want with me? I'm just a little tramp. You like me now, but you'll get tired. You'll be sorry you brought me. You'll be ashamed of me. Your family ain't going to like me.

DUTCH: Honey . . .

RITA (*Crying out*): Why should they like me? I'm a nothing! Give me a little more chance at my career, Dutch! If I was a star, then everybody would like me. Then I would go to St. Louis with you, and you'd see, all your friends would like me. See, then you could be proud of me. I know you'll leave me, Dutch. I know you will.

DUTCH (*Holding her now*): You're like a little baby.

RITA (*Weeping on his chest*): I'm sorry, Dutch. I'm sorry.

DUTCH (*With deep parental calm and affection*): Take it easy now. Take it easy.

RITA: I'm no good. I'm no good.

He holds her, rocking a little back and forth, patting her head gently, very much as if he were calming a frightened baby.

DISSOLVE TO *Exterior. The Westwood movie theater. Night.* LONG SHOT *looking toward the entrance of the theater. In the foreground stands a Santa Claus in shirt sleeves and red trousers, ringing a bell. This, and the fact that people on the sidewalks wear light topcoats, is the only indication that it is winter. Some people come out of the theater; two of them are Rita and Dutch. Camera pans with them as they come toward us and past us, long enough for us to see that much of the warmth of their earlier relationship has drained away*

over the months. They walk silently, not particularly in-
terested in each other, toward a Cadillac convertible
parked down the street a bit. She opens the door on her
side and gets in; he walks around to his side and gets in.

DISSOLVE TO *Exterior. En route back to their hotel.*
Night.

PROCESS TWO SHOT *as they drive along darkened*
Sunset Boulevard back to their hotel, the dark landscape
gliding along behind them, occasional cars on the high-
way. They sit silently, unrelated. Rita is looking vaguely
at the passing landscape. Dutch stares at the road ahead.

INTERIOR. *Lobby, Beverly Hills Hotel.* LONG SHOT
of Rita and Dutch coming into the lobby. It is deserted;
it is quite late at night. Dutch pauses at the desk for
messages; there are none. Rita waits in the middle of
the lobby for him to rejoin her. He goes to her and they
start wordlessly off for the elevators.

INTERIOR. *Their suite at Beverly Hills Hotel.* ME-
DIUM LONG SHOT *looking toward the door, which now*
opens; a shaft of hall light shoots into the black room.
Rita and Dutch are two black, bulky silhouettes in
the doorway for a moment. Then Dutch turns the en-
trance light on. He moves farther into the room, turning
on the room light and pocketing his key as he goes. Rita
closes the door and comes slowly into the room after

him. Dutch removes his coat, hangs it up in the closet, yawns, rubs the back of his neck. Rita goes to the window, closes the Venetian blinds. Dutch sits down on a soft chair, removes his shoes. Rita lets her cloth stole drop onto another chair, goes off to the bathroom, turns on the light, closes the door.

FULL SHOT of Dutch taking off his black silk socks now. He tucks them into his shoes, bends, picks the shoes up, stands, carries them to the side of the room, puts them down. Camera pans with him. He wriggles his arms free of his jacket, which he drops on a chair, and then slides out of his suspender straps.

CLOSE SHOT of Rita in the bathroom, surrounded by gleaming white tile. She is slipping out of her dress. She hangs it on a hook on the door. She is wearing a corsetlike undergarment with a starched underslip. She opens the door and calls dully out to her husband.

RITA: You want to give me my robe?

She leaves the door slightly ajar, sits down on the edge of the tub, begins ungartering her stockings. A moment later the bathroom door opens and her husband appears, proffering a pink lace peignoir. She takes it from him without rising and lets it fall loosely over the edge of the tub, so that the sleeves and collar form a soft puddle on the bottom of the tub. She goes back to ungartering her stockings, looks up, notes her husband, now in undershirt and trousers, standing, looking at her. She looks down at her other stocking and starts to ungarter that. After a moment she reaches over with one foot and closes the bathroom door in her husband's face. She strips off her second stocking and stands, leaving the two stockings in wispy heaps on the bathroom floor. She stands in front of the full-length mirror regarding herself with no evident expression. She reaches behind herself and begins to unhook the corsetlike undergarment.

FULL SHOT of Dutch in pajama bottoms moving back to the small entrance hallway to turn off the light there. His suit lies carelessly draped over the back of a soft chair. After he turns off the entrance light, he moves around the room, turning off the lamps, leaving only a reading lamp by the soft chair on which Rita's stole lies. He finds a copy of Life on the bed table between the twin beds, carries it to the soft chair, moves the stole aside, sits and begins thumbing through the magazine. He is a strong, lithe, muscular man, his chest thick with blond hair, somberly looking at the pictures in Life. After a moment the bathroom door opens and Rita appears, carrying her dress, which she throws over Dutch's suit on the soft chair. She is wearing the pink peignoir. She puts a handful of jewelry, a choker and a bracelet, on the chest of drawers, sits down on one of the twin beds and examines her fingernails. Dutch

*rises, comes over to her, sits down beside her, begins
kissing her neck.*

RITA *(Examining her nails):* Aren't you going to brush
   your teeth or wash up or anything?

*Dutch rises a little sullenly and goes into the bath-
room, leaving the door ajar. Camera stays on Rita. She
lies back on the bed now and stares up at the ceiling.
Behind her, off screen, we hear the sound of rushing water, then off, and Dutch comes out of the bathroom,
stands looking down at her. She closes her eyes. He lies
down on the bed beside her, reaches over and grips her
limp body, and kisses her on the mouth. His face is emo-
tionless, even cold. His head moves to kiss her neck and
we see Rita's face close up over his shoulder. She is staring at the ceiling. Then her eyes close again, and she
prepares to suffer through the experience.*

DISSOLVE TO *Interior. The hotel room.* FULL SHOT
*of Dutch sleeping heavily on his twin bed. The room is
dark now except for the lights of the patio and the
moonlight, which brings a vague, white light into the
room, drawing a thin white outline along the furniture
pieces. Camera pans slowly across the room, noting that
the other bed has been occupied but is not now, and
eventually finding Rita sitting in the soft chair by the
now slightly opened Venetian blinds. She is wearing her
peignoir and smoking a cigarette, sipping a highball.*

The bottle of liquor is on the chest of drawers at her elbow. She is a little drunk. She is staring bleakly down at the carpeting.

DISSOLVE TO *Interior. Their hotel suite.* FULL SHOT *of Dutch standing in his pajama trousers, unshaven for two days, hair unkempt; he has obviously just awakened and not from a particularly good sleep. His eyes are slitted with cold fury, and he is brandishing a magazine.*

DUTCH: You have to pose for these kind of pictures!

He flings the magazine in the direction of the bathroom door. It flaps against the wall and slithers to the floor. Rita is standing in the bathroom doorway. She wears an overly chic cocktail dress, which is still unzipped under her armpits and hangs loosely about her. She has not put on her shoes yet and stands in her stocking feet. She is fixing her hair, which is loose. There is a slatternly feeling about her. She is in a sullen rage herself.

RITA: I didn't know he was going to sell them to that magazine. He told me the pictures were for *Esquire.*

He turns away, his anger thick within him, an inarticulate, unexplored anger, really against himself, but no less intense for that. He sits down in the soft chair,

*stares at his toes, absently rubs his unshaven cheeks.
Rita has gone back into the bathroom. We can see her
from the back, standing in front of the wall mirror over
the basin, angrily bobby-pinning her hair. She turns
now, comes back to the open doorway, surveys her husband with sullen distaste.*

RITA: You coming with me or not?

DUTCH: Where?

RITA: You know where.

DUTCH: I never know where you go any more.

RITA: Lester Brackman is giving a party because they
finished shooting the picture this morning. Lester
Brackman says my bit was the stand-out bit of the
whole picture. He told me R. M. Lucas, Vice Presi-
dent in Charge of Production, saw the rushes, says
I'm going to steal the whole picture. They're having
a party on the set. Are you coming?

*Dutch says nothing, sits heavily in swollen, dull
anger. Rita waits for an answer. Then, still fixing her
hair, she moves across the room, a little squatly in her
stocking feet. She opens a closet door.*

RITA: I don't like this dress. I'm going to change it.
Draw the blinds, Dutch.

DUTCH: What for? All anybody has to do is buy that
magazine.

She turns and regards her husband with cold dislike.

RITA: I never cheated on you once, Dutch, in the eleven months we've been married. Not even for business. I could have had a contract with Lester Brackman a hundred times. All I had to do was say a word. But I told him, "Mr. Brackman, I'm a married woman. I don't do that kind of thing any more." I never cheated on you once. That's more than you can say.

The point is a telling one. He looks away.

RITA: Just don't cheat with girls I know, Dutch, because it gets back to me.

She zips her dress with angry, sharp movements of her hands, finds a pair of shoes lying on the carpeting by the closet door, straightens them with her toe, slides her feet into them.

RITA: Why don't you shave? You haven't been out of this room in two days. You better get a hold of yourself. You sleep till one, two o'clock every day now.

She crosses coldly back to the bathroom, stands in front of the bathroom mirror, examining herself. The basin below the mirror is covered with endless jars of

*cosmetics and lipstick tubes. In the living room, Dutch
sits sullenly, thickly.*

DUTCH *(Eyes down, muttering):* Maybe if I had a wife
who was a wife . . . *(Looks up as Rita starts back
into the room)* You don't care about me. You never
cared about me. *(His voice has begun to rise)*

RITA *(Her own voice suddenly shrill):* Any time you
wanted me, I submitted to you.

*They are suddenly shouting at each other, drown-
ing out each other's words.*

DUTCH: Oh, shut up!

RITA: Why don't you leave me alone?

DUTCH: Shut up! Shut up! Shut up!

RITA: You sit there watching television all night long.

DUTCH: You married me to get your name in the papers!

RITA: Why'd you marry me?

DUTCH: Two-bit tramp!

RITA: I never understood that! Just tell me!

DUTCH: I have to send my own clothes to the cleaners!

RITA: Just tell me that!

DUTCH *(Crying out):* What? What? What do you want?

RITA *(Staring out the window):* All right, quiet. Everybody'll hear you.

*He stands and moves quickly away because he is
horrified to find that he is about to cry.*

DUTCH (*Crying out*): Because I thought you was a nice girl! I thought you liked me!

He sits down on the bed. A cold, unresolved silence fills the room, a silence thick with hatred and unspoken violence.

DUTCH (*Mutters*): I'd like to get out of this town. I don't know what keeps me here. I don't know where to go. I don't know what to do.

Rita stands, much more deeply disturbed by their sudden flurry of hatred than she herself knows. She hopes he will continue talking, but he just sits, a somehow disheveled and beaten man, frightened even to look at the intense, flinty woman he has married. After a moment she says:

RITA (*Hoping he will agree*): You coming or not? I'll wait for you if you want to get dressed.

He says nothing, stares at the floor. She stands, her entire body taut with the feeling of her trapped marriage, aching to leave with some feeling of resolution but completely unequipped to deal with the matter. After a moment she turns and takes two steps toward the door and then stops.

RITA: I'm going. Okay?

He says nothing. She turns wearily and goes out the door.

Dutch stands promptly upon the closing click of the door, walks a few aimless paces around the room. He turns and shuffles barefoot to the telephone table between the beds, perches on the welter of bedsheets and blankets on one bed, lifts the phone, waits.

DUTCH *(Muttering into phone)*: You got any messages for me? . . . Okay . . . Yeah, yeah, will you get Mr. Kleiner for me, please? Thanks. . . . Sports desk, please. . . . Hello, Allie, this is Dutch. I got a message you called me. . . . No, I just woke up. . . . No, I don't want to go. . . . Ah, I feel lousy. . . . I don't know, I just feel like sitting around the room. . . . She went to a party down at the studio. They just finished her picture. . . . What do I want to go to the fights for? . . . Who else is going? . . . Ah, they'll just keep asking me who's better, Canzoneri or Barney Ross. . . . Listen, whyn't you bring them over here and we'll watch it on TV or something. . . .

DISSOLVE TO *Interior. Hotel suite, living room.* WIDE GROUP SHOT *showing Dutch Seymour and three other men in the living room of Dutch and Rita's hotel suite. The first man is fifty-odd, the second man forty-*

*odd. They are both unmistakably of pugilistic back-
ground, a little given to weight. The third man is a
reasonably intelligent-looking fellow—a newspaperman.
They are involved in one of those endless, familiar bull
sessions that ex-boxers fall into. They are all vaguely
bored, but this is all they have to talk about. They have
heard the stories a hundred times, but they still summon
enough energy to laugh. Dutch is removed from it all—
detached from the talk, bored by the baseball game
showing on the television set, deep within his own
pained thoughts.*

SECOND MAN: You guys remember Baldy Hoffman?

FIRST MAN: Baldy Hoffman? Hey, Dutch, I ever tell
you, Dutch—hey, Dutch—about the time, Dutch—
hey, Dutch—about the time Baldy Hoffman was
fighting Oscar the Turk? Hey, Dutch, he was no
more a Turk than you or me, Dutch. Hey, Dutch, he
was an Irishman from Fall River, Mass.

SECOND MAN: You guys remember Baldy Hoffman with
those big feet of his?

FIRST MAN: Used to fight 1921, 1922, around that time.
He had hair all over him. He looked like a gorilla.

SECOND MAN: Hey, Rocky, you mind if I tell a story?

FIRST MAN: What? What?

SECOND MAN: I can't get a word in edgewise with this
guy here.

FIRST MAN: Hey, Dutch . . .

Dutch turns a dutiful interest to the persistent sound of his name.

FIRST MAN: I ever tell you, Dutch, about the time Baldy Hoffman—he got the biggest feet in Boston, you know—I ever tell you guys—hey, Dutch, I ever tell you guys about the time Baldy Hoffman, he can't find his fighting shoes?

The other two men have begun to laugh. The second man, who has heard this story endless times already, begins rocking back and forth in his seat, shaking with silent merriment.

FIRST MAN: Well he can't borrow a pair. Man, there's nobody in Boston gotta pair o' shoes Baldy can wear. So he has to fight barefooted. By the third round he got so many blisters from the canvas, Dutch—hey, Dutch—he gotta cool off his feet in a pail of water, Dutch. Hey, Dutch . . .

Everybody but Dutch is absolutely choking with laughter now.

FIRST MAN (*Roaring with laughter himself*): Hey, Dutch, that Baldy, he got such big feet he can't get them in the pail!

Dutch works up a thin smile for the story.

FIRST MAN (*He can hardly get the words out, he is laughing so much*): He says, "Hey! I can't get my feet inna pail!" (*Screams of laughter*) He finally gets one of his feet in, he can't get the foot out!

This is too much for Second Man. He gets up and walks around in little circles, clutching his aching sides. Dutch abruptly stands.

DUTCH: I don't feel so hot. You guys stay here.

He turns sharply and exits. The laughter drains out of the others. The newspaperman regards the departing Dutch with a frown.

DISSOLVE TO *Interior. A sound stage.* ANGLE SHOT *looking down on a movie sound stage. There is an after-picture party going on. An improvised buffet has been set up on two carpenter's horses, and about thirty people stand loosely around in the huge, sprawling area, holding drinks and paper plates covered with cold cuts, murmuring, occasionally laughing. Most of the party are crew members and are in their shirt sleeves and work clothes. There are about eight or nine women; a few men in jackets and neckties. It is not a particularly gay affair.*

FULL SHOT *of Dutch picking his way past a flat and*

joining the large opened area where the party is quietly going on. He stands on the fringe, watching the party.

DUTCH'S POV: *The desultory party. At the far end of the long shot we see Rita gaily chatting with two men wearing jackets and ties. She holds a drink. She has noted Dutch's entrance. She is one of those girls who always have one eye on the entrance to see who's coming. When she thinks she has caught Dutch's eye, she smiles and waves a little. He does not respond; instead, he turns away and moves a few paces to an impeccably dressed man in his late forties with an intelligent but determinedly sardonic face. The man is talking to another man in shirt sleeves. He watches Dutch approach with a smile.*

DUTCH: Hello, Lester, how are you?
BRACKMAN: Hello, Dutch. Want a drink?

Dutch shakes his head. Lester returns his attention to the man he is talking to.

BRACKMAN: Well, I don't know, Joe. I think you'll be free by the end of the week. It looks pretty good to me. Maybe one, two days of retakes. We'll know that by Wednesday.
DUTCH: Lester . . . *(Brackman bends to hear Dutch's muttered words)* Lester, my wife got any talent at all?

BRACKMAN: Well, she's got something, Dutch. She's very good in this picture. She's going to attract a lot of attention. She's got what I call the quality of availability. She's not particularly pretty. It's a kind of warmth that some women have that makes all the men in the audience think they could make her if they only knew her. She don't act—she's no Olivia de Havilland—but there's a lot of big stars in this town who ain't Olivia de Havilland. If you're asking me as a producer whether I think she's going to get somewheres, I'd say yeah, I'd like to sign her. You know, we've been getting about five or six hundred letters a week on this girl on her last picture. And the fan magazines are picking her up. There's apparently something about your wife, Dutch. R. M. Lucas saw her dailies. He's very excited about her. He wants to sign her, do a lot of publicity, a whole campaign.

DUTCH (*Without looking at the man*): Lester, I understand you're trying to make my wife. I'll bust your head open if I hear that again.

He turns and moves slowly off, picking his way past the flat he passed coming in. Lester Brackman stands pursing his lips.

DISSOLVE TO *Interior. A movie.* CLOSE SHOT *of Dutch sitting in the darkened movie theater. The diffuse gray light emanating from the screen far up ahead makes changing shadows on his face. He is watching the picture expressionlessly. Then his attention wanders downward and he stares at the back of the seat in front of him.*

DISSOLVE TO *Exterior. Santa Monica Boulevard. Night.* LONG ANGLE SHOT *looking down on the deserted boulevard at one o'clock in the morning. An occasional car shoots by. Otherwise, the dusky little shop fronts are empty and dark and bare. We see Dutch walking slowly, almost purposelessly, down the street. Camera waits for him to pass it. He gets near enough for us to see he carries a dull weight of pain inside him, and the ever-controlled muscles of his face are released enough to show this.*

DISSOLVE TO *Interior. Lobby, Beverly Hills Hotel.* LONG SHOT *showing Dutch slowly crossing the deserted lobby on his way to the elevators.*

DISSOLVE TO *Interior. Dutch and Rita's suite.* ME-DIUM LONG SHOT *looking toward the entrance door, which opens. Dutch's bulky silhouette blocks the light issuing from the hallway. The room itself is dark. With a sudden rush, Rita is upon him, flinging her arms around his neck and pressing herself to him.*

CLOSE TWO SHOTS *Rita and Dutch clutching each other in the opened doorway of their suite. The sudden unexpected explosion of love from his wife has ripped the last of Dutch's reserve away. He stares over his wife's head, tears rolling slowly out of wide-opened eyes. He presses his wife to him slowly, his cheek against the softness of her hair. Their words come in mumbles and whispers and with great effort.*

DUTCH: I want to go back to St. Louis, Rita. I want to go back to St. Louis.
RITA: I love you, Dutch. I love you. I love you.
DUTCH: Please come with me. Please . . .
RITA: Anything you say, Dutch.
DUTCH: Holy Jesus, Mary, Mother of Christ . . .

They hold each other in desperate embrace.

DISSOLVE TO *Interior. The hotel suite. Dawn.* FULL SHOT *of Rita and Dutch sleeping in their respective beds. It is dawn now, and the room is alight but gray. Dutch's robe lies on the floor in front of his bed. One of the bed pillows is on the soft chair. The bedspreads have been piled loosely on other chairs. Dutch sleeps peacefully on his side. Rita sleeps rigidly, her face almost stiff with control. Her sheets are twisted and one of the blankets is half off the bed. Suddenly she sits bolt upright, her eyes wide, staring. For a moment she just sits this way. Then she gets her feet over the side and sits holding her face in her hands and shaking her head as if to clear it of its suddenly turbulent thoughts. She gets up. She is wearing pajamas now, and she pads barefoot to the window and looks out on the dawning day. Then she turns and looks at her husband, a blanketed hump, one hairy bare arm over the covers, his face pressed deep in the pillows. She stares at him for a long moment, then sits down on a soft chair on top of a piled bedspread. She seems exhausted. Her shoulders slump wearily and her hands fall slackly between her knees. She stares abjectly at the floor.*

DISSOLVE TO *Interior. The hotel suite. Morning.* MEDIUM SHOT *looking across Rita's shoulders, sitting as she was in the last shot, toward Dutch's bed. He is just waking up. He shifts under his covers and eventually opens his eyes. After a moment, he sits up, dressed only in pajama bottoms. The sun is bright in the room. He looks quickly over to Rita sitting in the chair and knows instantly that whatever moment they had the night before has gone. He looks back at the floor, assembling himself, a chill gathering in his stomach.*

FULL SHOT *of Rita in the chair. Expressionless.* FULL SHOT *of Dutch standing now. He shuffles around the bed, past Rita, and pads off to the bathroom. He tries a quick look at his wife again and then goes into the bathroom. He closes the door.*

FULL SHOT *of Rita getting to her feet with some effort. Her mind is going lickety-split. Her face is one large frown of concentration as she assembles her words, arguments, points of discussion. She moves to the closed bathroom door, takes another moment to think. Then she says:*

RITA *(To the bathroom door):* Dutch, let's stay here just another couple of weeks. What's another couple of weeks? Lester Brackman wants me to come over to his office this morning. I'm entitled to my chance. We could live in St. Louis. I would make a two-picture deal and just fly out here to make the pictures. But we could live in St. Louis.

The sound of rushing water in the bathroom interrupts her. She turns a little, exasperated, sits on her bed by the bathroom door, waits till the sound of water stops.

RITA *(Suddenly crying out):* Dutch! I can't live in St. Louis and just be a nothing! I can't! You'll be tired of me in three months! You'll be sorry you brought me! I ain't no housewife. I wouldn't know what to do in a kitchen! I'll go crazy there, doing nothing all day long. I'm sorry, Dutch! I swear I'm sorry! I don't know why you put up with me at all!

Only silence greets her from behind the bathroom door. She waits a moment, then turns and begins to pace restlessly around. As she starts to say something, she becomes aware of muffled sounds behind the door. After a moment, she realizes that her husband is crying, and the sounds are deep, shuddering sobs. She wheels away from the door, clutching her hands, her face screwed into the most intense expression of pain. She stands, her eyes squeezed tight, every feature twisted into an agony she couldn't explain herself. Behind her, her husband's sobs come clearly through the door.

DISSOLVE TO *Exterior. Street in a major studio. Day.* HIGH ANGLE SHOT *looking down on the deserted studio street. The street is absolutely empty except for Rita striding briskly across the street from the blazingly bright side into the deep shadow cast by one of the executive buildings. She is overdressed just a little, as usual, everything a little too tight. She is the same brassy little starlet we met at the beginning of this part of the story.*

DISSOLVE TO *Interior. Brackman's reception room.* WIDE SHOT *showing Rita sitting composed and stiff on a wooden chair and a bespectacled secretary busy tapping away at her desk. It is the same sort of reception room that Burt Harres had except there is more of everything, including space and awards and picture posters hanging on the wall. Rita is the only one waiting. The intercom buzzes on the secretary's desk. She picks up one of the three phones on her desk, nods, looks at Rita.*

SECRETARY: You can go in, Miss Shawn.

The secretary puts the receiver back on the hook, returns to her typing. Rita rises and crosses to the door leading to the inner office.

INTERIOR. *Brackman's office.* FULL SHOT *of Rita entering, closing the door behind her.*

REVERSE SHOT. *The office is a corner one, obviously a prominent producer's office. It is done in the most impeccable taste. It is unbearably well furnished. Lester Brackman stands at a window. There is a man in his late sixties, portly, bland, pince-nezed, wearing a baggy blue suit with a vest, standing at the other window. An extremely large desk, covered with all the evidence of a busy producer carefully arranged all over it, dominates the center of the room.*

RITA *(Smiling at Lester):* Hello, Lester.

The two men smile at her.

BRACKMAN *(Detaching himself from his window):* Rita, I don't have to tell you who this is. *(He indicates the sixty-five-year-old man)* This is Mr. R. M. Lucas, one of our vice-presidents.
RITA: I'm very honored to meet you, sir.

BRACKMAN: Mr. Lucas saw the picture last night. He's very excited about your little scene.

Having concluded the introductions, Brackman retires diplomatically into a corner of the office, perches out of the way on a radiator cover. Mr. Lucas regards Rita blandly out of pale-blue eyes.

LUCAS: You're a very attractive girl. You screen very well. You're a strange type, but you're exciting. Audience response to you has been very interesting. Martin Charles, your director, says you have real talent. We think you're going to be very big. Got a very nice part for you, six weeks' work. Your agent will tell you to jump at it. Give Lester his name. We'll send him a script. We'd like to have you under contract, young lady. We'll make very nice terms for you. Why don't you come to my house tonight? We'll discuss the whole matter.

A thin smile forms on Lester Brackman's saturnine face.

LUCAS: I eat at eight o'clock. I'm sure you'll enjoy the food.

Rita looks knowingly at the old man, a little wearily.

RITA: Shall I dress or is it informal?

LUCAS: What does it matter? Mr. Brackman will give you the address. Give my best to your husband. A very fine fellow.

Rita, dismissed, smiles, turns, and goes out the door. A moment's pause hangs between the two men. Mr. Lucas regards his broad-toed shoes. Mr. Brackman exhales a breath of smoke. After a moment, Mr. Brackman makes a wry face and says:

BRACKMAN: A star is born.

FADE OUT.

Fade in *on Exterior. Street in Bel Air. Day.* Long, slow pan shot *panning across a rolling expanse of a house in Bel Air. The house is Spanish Monterey style, surrounded by flowering gardens, with a curved drive-way leading to and away from the high, heavy oak front door. It is obviously a big house, a rich house, a high-style house. Over this, the following legend:*

PART THREE

Portrait of a Goddess

Interior. *Rita's home. Several shots showing the large entrance foyer reaching two stories up, with a wide, curved stairway leading up to the second floor and a huge crystal chandelier dangling from the second-floor ceiling; the very large, rather old-fashioned kitchen with wall refrigerators, and a Negro man and a woman, middle-aged, working at the preparation of a meal.* Long shot *looking out the lanai windows, out across the flat red stones of the patio, the outdoor furniture, across a large expanse of green terrace that slopes down to a white Grecian colonnade and then to the pool. The whole area is surrounded by flower gardens, in which an occasional spouting statue stands. Over this, the following legend:*

HOLLYWOOD, CALIFORNIA—
1952

EXTERIOR. *Back terrace of Rita's home. Day.* LONG SHOT *showing a man and a woman coming out of the den doors onto the patio and starting across the long green terrace toward the pool. The man is tall, grayhaired, casually dressed. The woman is in her late thirties, chic in a casual summer dress and high heels.*

FULL SHOT *of the couple, whose name is Woolsy, reaching the white Greek banister and railing that separate the terrace from the pool. They wave to the lovely blond young woman sitting on a beach chair at the pool, who now stands to greet them. This is Rita Shawn, 1952, twenty-six years old, bronzed under the California sun, her hair a gleaming ashen blond, her body full in the white bathing suit. Behind her the undisturbed waters of the pool glisten green in the sunlight. Sitting erectly in a white wrought-iron chair is her mother, soberly dressed in a simple, formless print dress, bespectacled, reading. The mother is now forty-eight. A stern face, austerely pale, as if every instinct in her is resisting the sun.*

ANOTHER SHOT *favoring Rita as the Woolsys come down to the pool. We are aware now of edges of restlessness in Rita. She seems to be in constant small movement, a flicking of her cigarette, a crossing of her legs, sitting, standing, moving nervously about. Her eyes shift incessantly to the pool, to the fringe of high palms surrounding the gardens, to the baked red tiles at her feet, to whoever is talking. When she talks, there is an urgency in her words, as if she is not sure she is making her meaning clear. We see the vague harrows of troubled nights turning down the corners of her mouth and shadowing her eyes. One gets the feeling of a looseness of flesh, of too full a bosom, of long formless days of drinking and deep, gray mornings of despair. She is delighted to be roused from the silence that had hung between herself and her mother. She is on her feet instantly, in the furious flurry of introductions.*

RITA: This is my mother, Mrs. Faulkner. This is Mr. and Mrs. Joe Woolsy. Joe and Sally Woolsy. My mother just came in yesterday.

MRS. WOOLSY: Isn't that wonderful? How do you do.

The mother smiles and nods, looks up from her book.

RITA: My mother read in the paper how I had my

nervous breakdown, and she called me long distance. Well, I told you, I had that long talk with
my mother—it cost eighty-one dollars, that one call
—well, I told you all that, about her coming out
here.

MRS. WOOLSY: How long do you intend staying, Mrs.
Faulkner?

RITA: Well, she thinks she's just out here for a couple
of weeks, but she's really here to stay, because this
is her home from now on. I been trying to get her
out of that little old shack—she lives with my aunt
and uncle—for years, and now that I got her out
here, I ain't going to let her go. Ma, Mr. Woolsy is
the producer of the picture on which I had my
breakdown, and they been at my side all through
the experience. They are my oldest and dearest
friends. I thought I had a lot of friends, but these
two here visited me every day at the sanitarium,
and they were the only two, I might add. Except
Shirley Donehoe. She's my hairdresser. She's been
my hairdresser on every picture since 1949. I
wouldn't do a picture without her. But all my other
so-called friends, why, they didn't know I was alive,
which just goes to show you something. I don't
know what. Why don't you all sit down?

MRS. WOOLSY: Well, actually, we just stopped by to
see if you would have lunch with us. We're going
to—

RITA: Well, I just think I'll stay here and have lunch

with my mother. I haven't seen her in eight years. Eight years! My heavens, that's no way for a mother and daughter to be. Did I tell you, Abe Silverman called in a state yesterday. He just found out I wasn't seeing that psychiatrist any more.

MRS. WOOLSY: Yes, we know.

RITA: I said, "Abe, I'm not crazy. I don't need any psychiatrist." Why don't you all stay with us for lunch?

MRS. WOOLSY: No, Rita dear, we—

RITA (*Starting abruptly for the stairs to the terrace*): I'll go tell the cook that—

MRS. WOOLSY: Rita, we're having lunch with Arlene Hugo at Frascati's.

RITA: Well, I'll go check and see what's holding it up anyways.

She hurries, in her almost frantic fashion, up the stairs and the green, neatly mowed terrace to the house. An uncomfortable pause falls between the Woolsys and the mother.

THE MOTHER (*After a moment*): I want to thank you for all you did for my daughter in her time of need. She speaks of your friendship with the deepest affection.

WOOLSY (*Frowning*): Mrs. Faulkner, we hardly know your daughter. I never met her till she was assigned to my picture four months ago. She only met my wife three weeks ago. I visited her at the sanitarium because she was holding up my picture for thirteen days. Cost me well over a hundred and fifty thousand dollars. It makes me very sad to feel she considers us her best friends. I think it's very good that you're out here, Mrs. Faulkner. I think she needs somebody very much. Try to talk her into going back to her psychiatrist.

THE MOTHER: Well, I'm sure I don't know.

WOOLSY: You talk to her, Mrs. Faulkner. She needs a psychiatrist. You talk to her.

DISSOLVE TO *Interior. Rita's home.* FULL SHOT *of Rita standing in the den dressed in a casual frock now, smoking a cigarette, giving a frowning but not really interested attention to the television set. The GOP political convention is going on. She moves nervously, restlessly around the room, dropping her ashes in various ash trays. Then she moves in her sandaled feet out into the main entrance foyer and then into the lanai, pausing a moment to look out through the windows across her patio and sloping green terrace. Her cigarette has been smoked down to the filter, and she turns and crushes it out in an ash tray on the lanai table. She promptly lights another one. She shuffles into the butler's pantry, where she smiles briefly at the woman servant, hard at work preparing dinner now. She peeks into the kitchen, which is empty.*

RITA *(To the woman servant):* How's everything?

The woman smiles. Rita moves with a brief sigh back into the lanai, back into the entrance foyer, and starts up the wide curved stairway. A Siamese cat slinks silently down the stairs past her.

INTERIOR. *Rita's home, upstairs landing.* FULL SHOT *of Rita coming to the top of the carpeted stairway, pausing a moment to look down the length of the corridor to her left.*

REVERSE SHOT *at the far end of the corridor. We can see into what seems to be a darkened bedroom—dark, that is, in relation to the brightness of the other rooms. Her mother is sitting, dressed as she was before, in a stiff armchair, reading her Bible. After a moment, Rita moves down the corridor to her mother.*

EXTERIOR. *The mother's bedroom.* ACROSS-THE-SHOULDER SHOT *over Rita's shoulder to her mother.*

RITA: How do you feel, Ma?

THE MOTHER: Oh, everything's just fine. This is about the biggest house I think I ever saw.

RITA: I guess you could put Mrs. Phillips' house on Union Street which she was so arrogant about right inside that living room.

THE MOTHER: I guess you could.

RITA: I made inquiries about an Adventist congrega-

tion here in Los Angeles, and there is one. I'll drive
you down there tomorrow.

THE MOTHER: Fine, because I do not want to miss Fri-
day-night Sabbath.

*Rita moves into the room, silently padding to the
opposing wall, and sits down on a second soft chair.*

RITA: You go on with your praying, Ma. I'll just sit here.

*The mother, who has already turned her attention
back to her Bible, her lips moving silently, smiles briefly
even as she prays. For a long, long moment the room is
hushed and still between the two women—the older
woman by the window, softly murmuring over the Scrip-
tures, the younger woman huddled in the far-corner soft
chair watching her with wide eyes.*

RITA (*Suddenly*): I make four thousand dollars a week.
Did I ever tell you that, Ma? You know what the
studio got for me when they lent me out to Colum-
bia for that Cary Grant picture? A quarter of a
million dollars, but they got me on that staff con-
tract, so all I got was my four thousand a week.
Did you see the latest *Film Daily* listings? Well,
I'm in the top eight in *Film Daily* box-office ratings.
Do you know the kind of business my last picture,
Stardust Girl, did on opening day in New York?
We opened at the Roxy in New York, and we did

fourteen thousand dollars, and that was a house record for an opening day. We did a boff one hundred and fifty-eight thousand for the week. What do you think of your little girl now?

THE MOTHER: Well, that's very nice.

RITA: What are you reading, Ma?

THE MOTHER (*Looks briefly at her Bible, then turns to her daughter and recites amiably from memory*): "And ye shall know that I am the Lord, when I have opened your graves, O my people, and brought you up out of your graves, and shall put my Spirit in you, and ye shall live, and I shall place you in your own land; then shall ye know that I the Lord have spoken it, and performed it, saith the Lord."

Tears well in Rita's eyes as she stares at her mother.

RITA: I'm so glad you came, Ma, because I was like to go crazy just wandering around this house all by myself.

THE MOTHER: I meant to come the day I read in the papers about your nervous breakdown, but the doctor—

RITA (*The words pour out of her*): I don't know what's the matter with me. I have these black moods when I'm like to kill myself. I'm really like to kill myself. I had this nervous breakdown. They tell me I began to scream right on the set about this cat. Somebody had brought a cat on the set, and I just began to scream to take it away from me. And I love cats. I got these two big Siamese—you seen them. But my nerves were at the breaking point. I'd been drinking heavily. I confess to the sin of drinking. Oh, my God, I was arrested twice for drunken driving. I just feel, Ma, I'm losing all control of myself. I feel I'm going crazy. Sometimes I wake up in the morning, I don't know what I done the night before, and I feel I'm going right out of my mind. I can't bear to be alone. I can't bear it. I've taken men home with me who I didn't rightly know for more than an hour because I can't bear to be alone at night. I wake up in the middle of the night in a sweat and my heart pounding, and I've gone down and awakened my servants and made them sit with me till morning. Life just seems unbearable to me. I need you, Ma. I need you to be here with me because I'm like to go insane. I feel I'm going insane.

THE MOTHER: We are all put on this earth to suffer.

RITA: I'm going to take care of you. Wherever I go. I'm going to take you with me. You will always be at my side.

THE MOTHER: I spoke to you on the phone last week, and I hung up, and I turned to Elliot Wainwright, who is an elder, and to your aunt, who was sitting there, and I said, "Riches and fame mean nothing, for here is my daughter, the envy of her generation, who like to cry her heart out over the phone. She is a lost soul, and all the glory of her life is just vanity. King Solomon had all the wealth of the world, and queens of mighty nations rode miles of sand and desert to see him, and what did he say but 'It is all vanity.' " I said, "My daughter is approaching her cataclysm. She has lived a life of sin and torment. She has borne the mark of the beast upon her. And surely she will be redeemed just as all men shall be redeemed from the curse as his corpse molders back to his mother earth."

She stands, stares at her daughter, her eyes wide with fervent intensity, but her words are gentle.

THE MOTHER: Wipe away the red stains of sin and clothe yourself in dignity. Your body is the temple of the Holy Spirit, and you must keep yourself in modesty. Let righteousness into you, honey. Open your soul, open your arms, and just let Jesus Christ in you. Don't hold back a thought. Just let Him fill your body and your soul, and ye shall be transported into Peace and Love. *(Her eyes are closed now as she experiences something of the rapture she describes)* O Lord, O Lord, I yield myself without reservation, and I feel the sweet, sweet warmth and peace.

In the corner soft chair, Rita sits hunched, bent almost double, stirred by some physical anguish she has

*never felt before. Her face is contorted with pain, her
eyes clenched shut, her knuckles white as her hands grip
each other.*

RITA (*Muttering*): I feel Him near me. I feel Him near
    me.
THE MOTHER: Without reservation. Ye must open your
    heart and your soul.
RITA: Oh, my God, my God!
THE MOTHER: Without reservation . . .
RITA: Oh, my God, my God!
THE MOTHER: Life is pain and sin and torment, and
    Jesus Christ absolves you, and there ain't no pain,
    and there ain't no sin, and there ain't no torment
    because your body is filled with His eternal love
    and His eternal compassion. Just open your arms
    and let Christ come in to every part of you.

*Suddenly Rita falls from her contorted position on
the soft chair onto the thickly carpeted floor, falling
softly on her knees, her back bent in an arch of trem-
bling and supplication. She is sobbing, rather from the
extraordinary exhilaration that suffuses her than from a
sense of pain. Her eyes are open, brimming with tears,
and she stares through the wet film of her tears at the
carpet before her. Her mother regards her with deep and
gentle compassion. She pads quietly to her daughter's
bent figure and strokes her hair. She kneels down beside
her and begins to pray quietly. Rita suddenly clutches*

at her mother, and the two women hold each other in passionate embrace.

Dissolve to Interior. Rita's home. Long shot looking straight at the heavy oaken front door of the house, which opens now to admit Rita with her mother right behind her. Rita seems in the best of spirits. She wears a sober dress and flat-heeled shoes. Her face is devoid of any make-up. She comes hurrying across the entrance hall to the lanai, calling:

Rita: Joe!

She crosses into the lanai to the screen doors leading out onto the patio.

Exterior. Rita's house, patio. Day. Full shot of Rita coming out onto the patio. Joe and Mrs. Woolsy are slouched on the porch furniture. They are reading newspapers and smoking. Woolsy stands as Rita comes out.

Rita: I'm sorry to be so late, but the time just flew. *(Calling back to the house)* We're out here, Ma. *(To the Woolsys)* I'll go check dinner. We went for a long ride. I took my mother out to Encino and Sherman Oaks. I showed my mother John E. Tower's home, the father of my first husband. I wonder who's living there now. They got some pretty big ranches out that way. We saw a pretty good-size herd of cattle. *(Looking at screen door)* I guess she went upstairs to wash.

WOOLSY: It's nice to see you looking so well, Rita.

RITA: Well, now, Joe, I'm happy. I have found God. I truly have. I tell this to you and Sally because I don't think you would mock me. But last Wednesday night, I woke up in the middle of the night with my old panic. Joe, you was at my side when I tried to kill myself on location in Arizona when I had my breakdown, so you know how I was. Well, Wednesday night, I woke up and went in to my mother and woke her up, and we prayed. I prayed to God to save my soul. I held my mother's hand. I remember her fingers tight on mine, and that's what saved me, her holding my hand that way. Because I can tell you now just what I feel when I have these nightmares and get drunk like I used to. It's the most awful loneliness in the world. I remember my first husband telling me about this awful loneliness he used to feel. Now, I know what he meant. It's like all the world is off somewheres else like an echo. It must be the loneliness a crying infant feels when it's left all alone. It's just so unbearable I can't describe it. And I remember holding onto my mother's hand and praying. And I tell you, it went away. I felt so light and relieved from pain and trouble. I couldn't sleep the rest of the night. I just sat with my mother, and we talked and

talked. And dawn came up—it was the most beautiful dawn, fiery red like flame, like God was saying
to me, "It's all right," like He personally was saying
that to me. And I like to burst, I felt so fine. Oh,
glory, it's so fine to have my mother with me!

*There is a radiance to her face now that deeply
touches her two friends.*

MRS. WOOLSY: Well, it's wonderful to see you this way,
     Rita.
RITA: I feel I'm ready to go back to work, Joe. I'm go-
     ing to call Abe Silverman and tell him to inform the
     studio I am ready to read any scripts they care to
     send me.

DISSOLVE TO *Exterior. Patio of Rita's home. Night.*
LONG SHOT *of the mother sitting alone on a straight-
backed, wrought-iron garden chair. It is not a rocker,
but the mother rocks lightly back and forth as if it were.
Her hands are folded in her lap. She is visible in the
dark summer night because the lights of the patio are
on. Around her, the night is still except for the chirp of
crickets.*

CLOSE SHOT *of the mother on the patio, rocking
back and forth. She is the picture of profound resigna-
tion, but her face is troubled. After a moment she stands,*

*frowning a little, and goes through the lanai screen
doors into the dark lanai.*

INTERIOR. *Rita's home, lanai.* FULL SHOT *of the
mother coming into the dark lanai, her outline visible
because of the patio lights and the lights in the butler's
pantry. She pauses a moment, framed against the lanai
windows, and then moves into the butler's pantry.*

INTERIOR. *The butler's pantry.* LONG SHOT *showing
the mother coming into the lighted pantry. The middle-
aged Negro cook is at the sink silently washing some
lettuce. The mother stands at the far end of the pantry,
watching her tentatively for a moment.*

THE MOTHER: Well, she's just coming home later and
later.
THE COOK: Sometimes she don't come home till eleven,
twelve o'clock at night when she's making a picture.
I can set your plate if you're hungry.
THE MOTHER: No, no. I'll just wait on my daughter.

*She looks down at the floor, stands, frowns. The
cook goes back to unleafing the lettuce.*

THE MOTHER: Well, maybe I'll just rustle myself up
something. Don't you pay no mind to me. I don't

feel comfortable having somebody serving me, waiting on me hand and foot. *(She's at the wall refrigerator, poking her head in, looking for some appetizer)* I do all my own cooking at home. I cook for my brother and my sister-in-law. I live with them. My brother George is more in bed than out, he is that sick, and my sister-in-law is at the store most of the day. We have a grocery and fruit store. I work there a couple of hours a day too. I have a very busy day back there in Beacon City. Sometimes I just drop in my bed exhausted at the end of the day. I'll just take some of this here cheese.

THE COOK: You go right ahead and take some of that cheese, ma'am.

The mother has found some American cheese. She unfolds a strip from the pack and nibbles at it.

THE MOTHER *(After a moment):* I'm so very lonely out here. I'm like to go out of my mind.

THE COOK: Well, it's hard to get to know somebody out here.

THE MOTHER: My daughter's away all day, and most of the night. She's gone at seven in the morning. I just walk around from one room to another. I just don't know what to do with myself. My daughter and I went down to a church meeting, but the congregation was mostly colored.

She bites her lip even as she says the words, morti-fied with embarrassment.

THE MOTHER: I didn't mean to say that.
THE COOK (*Dryly*): That's all right, Mrs. Faulkner.

An embarrassed silence falls between the two women for a moment.

THE MOTHER: I got another letter from my sister-in-law. They all miss me very much. She writes how the Schefflers—he's the cashier in the supermarket —and their two little boys was over the other night, and they was watching the boys catching fireflies. It's so lovely in Maryland about this time of year in the evening, and the smell of jasmine and honey-suckle is sweet enough to just breathe into your whole body. Oh, I do admit I am homesick. I just ache with it. It's awful hard for a woman of my years to just uproot herself and come live some-wheres else. I lived twenty-two years in Beacon City.
THE COOK: Well, it's hard to leave home, no matter how old you are.
THE MOTHER: Yes, it is.

There are tears in her eyes, and she turns away sadly and moves back into the dark lanai, nibbling on her cheese. She stands silhouetted against the windows of the lanai, an aging little woman with wet eyes.

DISSOLVE TO *Interior. The mother's room.* LONG SHOT *looking past Rita to the bathroom door. Rita still wears a sober dress and no lipstick. She seems in a temper. Her mother is just coming out of the bathroom, wiping her hands on a towel. She is dressed in what would seem to be her one dress, the formless print. Religious pictures and calendars have been pinned on the wall. There is one battered valise open on the bed.*

RITA *(Repressed fury):* I ain't going to pay your railroad fare. If you're thinking I'm going to pay your railroad fare back, you're crazy. I ain't even going to take you down to the station and buy you tickets. You just find your own way down to the station. I ain't going to send you no more money. I ain't going to send you nothing.

THE MOTHER: Honey, I told you when I first came out here—

RITA: All I know is—

THE MOTHER: I didn't expect I would stay more than two or three weeks.

RITA: I done everything I can to make you happy.

THE MOTHER: I been out here more than two months now.

RITA: I gave a ten-thousand-dollar tithe for the furthering of missionary work.

THE MOTHER: Honey, your Uncle George is more in bed than out, he is that sick, and Alice Marie tends the store, and they can hardly make do without me.

The feeling of some unexpressed hatred suffuses Rita's body in a wave of almost physical heat. Sweat appears in beads on her brow, and her face swells, and the words she says are bitten and unrestrained in their venom.

RITA *(Viciously):* Nothing I do pleases you. Nothing I ever did pleases you. All you know is to run off on me. I hate you so much I can't find words to tell you how much. You never cared whether I lived or died. Well, just get out of my house. I never want to see you again, not even in your grave. I hope your heart just explodes. I hope you die. I just want you to know that.

She turns on her heel and stalks out of the room. The mother stands with her head bowed, the towel hanging slackly from one hand, patiently resigned.

DISSOLVE TO *Interior. Rita's home, her bedroom.* FULL SHOT *of Rita standing by her bedroom window looking out through the white nylon curtains. The sun streams in, whitening her face.*

RITA'S POV: *Looking down to the front of the house.*

There is a Yellow Cab parked in the driveway in front of the big oaken door. The driver stands waiting for the mother to come out through the door, which is open. When the mother appears in her dark shapeless topcoat, the driver hurries to help her with her valise.

ANGLE SHOT *looking up past the driver as he loads the valise on and, as the mother gets into the cab, to Rita's window. She is desperately opening one of the casements of her window, pushing the curtains aside.*

RITA *(Screaming):* There ain't no God! You hear what I said? There ain't no God!

The driver nervously gets into his seat of the cab and starts the car quickly.

RITA *(Screaming):* There ain't no God! Can you hear me?

The taxi curves off down the driveway and wheels into the street and moves out of sight. Rita screams at its departing fumes of unburned oil.

RITA *(Screaming):* There ain't no God!

FULL SHOT *of Rita turning from the window. She sits down on a bedroom chair, slumped forward, her arms dangling between her knees, her eyes open, staring blankly at the wall ahead of her. She seems entirely spent, weary, exhausted. Suddenly one of her big Siamese cats swishes silently into the room and moves with feline restlessness around the room. Rita watches it expressionlessly. As it moves to rub against her leg, she reaches out and grabs it and presses it against her face.*

Close-up *of Rita's anguished face pressed against the endlessly smooth pale fur of the terrified cat.*

Rita *(Muttering to the cat):* There ain't no God.

The cat wriggles free and sprints out of the room. Rita remains seated, slumped and exhausted, devoid of any expression.

Fade out.

FADE IN *on Exterior. Beacon City, Maryland—1957.* VERY HIGH ANGLE SHOT *showing the whole town, lolling quietly on its hill on a hot August morning. The sun beats down on the sidewalks and most of the people are off in the shade of their homes and stores. Most of the people, that is, except for the seventy or eighty that are congregated outside a gray frame house on one of the hills. We may remember this to be the aunt's and uncle's home. There is also a number of cars lined up outside the home. Over this the following legend:*

BEACON CITY, MARYLAND—
1957

EXTERIOR. *Aunt's home. Day.* LONG SHOT AND CLOSER SHOTS *showing the crowd of people outside on the sidewalks, milling sweatily in the street, a shirt-sleeved crowd but quite respectful. There is no unruliness, just a quiet curiosity. It is apparently a funeral procession that is lined up on the street, for there are a hearse and two black limousines and seven other private cars. Suddenly there is a murmur and a press of movement in the people hanging around the house, and the pallbearers appear coming out of the front door bearing a coffin on their shoulders. They move slowly, sweating, down the front path to the hearse outside the house.*

The crowd is much more concerned with the people following the coffin out of the house—the elder, a spare young man in sober black suit, and then Rita Shawn in a black suit, black hat and veil, and black gloves. She seems faint, being held on one arm by her aunt, now a graying lady also in black, and on the other arm by a rather chic woman in her late forties wearing a blue suit.

FULL SHOT *of Rita being helped into the limousine by her aunt and the other woman. The elder stands by the open door of the limousine, watching them. After Rita is deposited in the car, he remarks to the woman in the blue suit, who stands wiping the sweat off her brow:*

THE ELDER: I hope all these people here believe she is grief-stricken, but God knows she came to her mother's funeral drunk as a lord.

THE SECRETARY: It's no sign of disrespect, Elder. She's always a little drunk. (*She climbs into the limousine*)

DISSOLVE TO *Exterior. Beacon City streets. Day.* SEVERAL SHOTS *showing various angles of the funeral procession wending its slow way through the town. On the hot sidewalks, a few hardy souls stand and watch; others look out of windows.*

INTERIOR. *The limousine. Group shot of the four occupants. Rita and her aunt sit in the rear seat. The elder and the secretary sit on the jump seats. The windows are all open, but the heat inside the car is oppressive. Rita stares through heavy-lidded eyes at the slowly passing store fronts of Main Street. Sweat gathers in beads on everyone's face. They ride stolidly, silently, squinting against the glaring blind spots on the shiny doors and chrome finishings. After a moment Rita, her voice slightly blurred, and without looking away from the passing scene, says:*

RITA: I just suddenly had a picture of myself twenty-five years ago, a little girl with high ankle shoes and a middy blouse, walking down the street here.

There are suddenly tears in her eyes, and she stares helplessly around her. Then she lapses back into her vague, lost study of the passing scene. The others ride silently. The aunt wipes her neck.

THE AUNT: My soul, it's hot.

They ride slowly on.

DISSOLVE TO *Exterior.* Cemetery. LONG SHOT *showing the funeral procession pulling to a halt outside the iron-railing fence of the cemetery. There is a crowd on the walk outside the cemetery, perhaps a hundred and fifty people. It parts into a respectful path for the transference of the coffin into the cemetery. There are six or seven people already waiting on a small knoll by an open grave. The fresh earth is piled on either side of the grave. The air is humid and dense. The people get out of the cars, form a disorganized line behind the four pallbearers and straggle through the headstones of the small cemetery to join the small group waiting at the grave. Among this group there is a thin, graying man in his late thirties and a girl of thirteen. We may recognize the man as John Tower, Jr. As they come close to him and the girl, he says:*

TOWER: Hello, Emily Ann.

Something in the quiet greeting frightens her, and she whirls to the voice. For a moment she just stares at Tower, and then the shock of recognition floods over her face. Then she says, quite in control of herself:

RITA: Hello, John. I hardly expected you here. John, you remember my aunt Alice Marie, and this is my secretary, Miss Haywood. This is my first husband, Mr. Tower. Will you excuse us, please?

They all nod their greetings. The secretary seems particularly hostile. Rita, supported by the two women, moves on farther to the grave into which the coffin is now being lowered. There is a moment of silence.

CLOSE SHOT *of Rita flanked by her aunt and secretary standing by the grave. All around her are grave-*

stones and crosses. The sun beats down on her. She moves her veil down over her face, and then darts a quick look back to Tower and the girl.

RITA'S POV: *Tower and his daughter, a not particularly distinguished-looking girl of thirteen among the fifteen-odd people around the grave. Over this shot, the elder begins his reading from the Bible, quiet and sonorous.*

ACROSS RITA'S SHOULDER *looking across the elder reading, past Tower and the daughter, past the rows of gravestones, to the hundred and fifty-odd people staring at her through the iron railings of the fence.*

CLOSE SHOT *of Rita, rubbing her eyes against the heat, the elder's words droning on behind her. Beside Rita we see the aunt's bowed head, the ever-present background of gravestones. The heat is beginning to get to Rita. Her eyes close, and her head shakes a little. Suddenly she begins to wail, screaming out into the hot afternoon sky:*

RITA: I want to die! I want to die! I can't stand it no more! I can't stand it! Leave me alone! I want to die!

The secretary moves quickly, slaps Rita sharply. Rita's panic abruptly subsides and her knees buckle.

The secretary is holding her tightly and preventing her from falling. A murmur rustles through the crowd outside the gate. The elder pauses in his reading. The secretary and the aunt, aided by one of the pallbearers, manage to move Rita away from the grave and back to the entrance of the cemetery.

LONG SHOT *looking past Tower and the daughter as Rita is being helped away. We can see enough of their faces to see the sad compassion on Tower's face and the wide-eyed fascination on the daughter's.*

DISSOLVE TO *Exterior. Porch of aunt's home. Dusk.* MEDIUM LONG SHOT *of the secretary and the aunt rocking quietly on the porch. The secretary has taken off her jacket and unbuttoned her blouse collar. There is still a curious group of about twenty people, mostly teen-agers, straggled along the sidewalk across from the house.*

LONG SHOT *of Tower coming up the street to the house, opening the gate and walking up the path to the porch.*

THE AUNT: Come on up here in the shade.

Tower climbs slowly up to the porch.

THE AUNT: I never expected to see you here.
THE SECRETARY (*With evident coldness*): Neither did I.

THE AUNT: It was very nice of you and the girl to come to the funeral.

TOWER: My daughter wanted very much to come.

THE SECRETARY *(Coldly):* She's asleep, Mr. Tower. I gave her some pills, and she went off.

TOWER: Do you think she'd like to see us?

THE SECRETARY: Not after the last time.

TOWER: My daughter would like to meet her very much.

THE SECRETARY: I don't think I'll let you see her, Mr. Tower.

TOWER *(Smoking nervously):* I'm not sure just what you have to say about all this, Miss Haywood.

THE SECRETARY: I've been with Miss Shawn for three years; I'm very fond of her. If there's anything that'll stay in my mind till the day I die, it's that picture of you sitting in that lawyer's office two years ago while that hysterical woman pleaded with you on her knees to see her daughter, and you just kept saying, "No."

TOWER: I didn't think it was a good idea for my daughter to spend two weeks with a hysterical woman.

THE SECRETARY: You destroyed that poor girl, Mr. Tower. You—

TOWER: She was destroyed long before then.

THE SECRETARY: Did you know she tried to kill herself that night?

TOWER: Miss Haywood, this is none of your business. *(He scowls, nervously crushes his cigarette out with his foot)* It is your job, Miss Haywood, to hover over that poor desolate woman upstairs. My job is to give my daughter some love of life. I don't really care about Rita Shawn any more. Or myself. We are a gutted generation, born in the depression and obsessed with prosperity. Well, we got prosperity, and what have we got? A hysterical woman upstairs who needs barbiturates to put her to sleep, Dexedrine Spansules to wake her up, and tranquilizers to keep her numb, who has a nervous breakdown once a year and has tried to kill herself at least four times that the public knows. I don't want my daughter to grow up like that. Or like me. A twisted, loveless man, patched together by psychoanalysis. My daughter was a very strange little girl for a long time, well on her way to continuing the desolate pattern of her parents, her grandparents, and all the generations before her, the long parade of history that has brought us to this year of suicide and insanity. Do you think I would take this frightened little girl and send her for two weeks with a meaningless mother, to be devoured by this wandering panther of a woman as she prowls through life looking for some reason for living? My daughter has a reason for living. She's not going to scream out in a hot cemetery that she wants to die. She wants to see her mother very much. She is a sweet girl. She has given me the little importance in life that I have. I thought she might give Rita a little of that.

THE SECRETARY: You worry about your girl, Mr. Tower. I'll worry about mine.

TOWER *(Murmurs):* So she finally found a mother. *(Takes out his cigarette pack to light another)* I'll come back later.

THE SECRETARY *(Frowns):* You might as well sit here. She'll be up soon. I better go upstairs. She likes me to be in the room when she wakes up.

She turns and goes back through the screen door into the house. Tower finds a chair on the porch and sits, loosening his collar.

DISSOLVE TO *Interior. Upstairs bedroom.* CLOSE SHOT *of Rita asleep on the bed. The shades are drawn, and the room is hushed and quiet. It is the same room she slept in when her mother first brought her to this house twenty-seven years ago. Camera dollies back to show the whole room. An electric fan whirs silently, fluttering the white lace fringes on the bed. Rita lies sleeping sweetly, like a child. Sitting perched on the window sill is the secretary, quietly studying the lovely blond girl on the bed in her long, white, childlike nightgown. After a moment Rita opens her eyes and lies without movement, looking vaguely up at the ceiling. From the small portion of the window not covered by the shade we can see that it is getting dark outside.*

THE SECRETARY (*Gently*): Hello, baby.

Rita turns her head on the pillow and regards her secretary.

RITA: Let's get out of here.

THE SECRETARY: We don't have to be back on the Coast till Monday.

RITA: Let's just get out of this town. I've been sick ever since we got here.

THE SECRETARY: Okay. We can take the eleven-o'clock flight to New York. Your husband, Mr. Tower, is downstairs.

RITA: Is the girl with him?

THE SECRETARY: No.

RITA: Okay, let him come up. What time is it?

THE SECRETARY: About a quarter to eight.

RITA: Give me a drink.

THE SECRETARY: I want you to eat something first.

RITA: Okay. Confirm those reservations. I want to get out of here. I feel I'm getting nervous again.

THE SECRETARY: All right, baby. Take it easy.

RITA (*Panic rising in her*): We never should have come here. We never should have come here.

THE SECRETARY (*Sharply*): Rita!

The little flurry of panic subsides. The secretary stands, crosses to the old-fashioned chest of drawers, opens her large shoulder bag, takes out a medicine bottle.

THE SECRETARY (*Unscrewing cap of bottle*): Do you want a pill if you're going to see your husband? (*She lets a flat capsule fall into her palm*) There's a condolence telegram came for you from Joe and Sally Woolsy.

RITA: Who are they? Oh, yeah. Whatever happened to them? (*She suddenly begins to cry*) Oh, I don't know, I don't know. (*She lies on the bed, a handsome blond woman, childlike in a long white cotton nightgown, crying quietly*) We never should have come here, Horty. It's the same old town, the same old town. You'd have thought it would have changed in thirteen years. But just some more cars and a couple of new neons, and the dime store got a new front window, but it's all the same. It's worse, even. I always thought this house was a pretty house, but it's a shabby old place, a shabby, shabby little wooden house. Did you see that place where I used to live? Oh, my God! It was an ugly, ugly childhood. Ugly and dirty and lonesome. Oh, my God! I can feel it now! That lonely little girl with her high ankle shoes! Oh, I don't know. Life never changes. I'm the same as I was then, and I'll always be the same, the same miserable little girl wandering through ugly streets in her high ankle shoes. I wish I could just sleep the rest of my life.

She is crying quite fully now. The secretary, who has listened patiently, even compassionately, now brings Rita the tranquilizer pill and a glass of water that was sitting on the chest of drawers. Rita gets up on one elbow, takes the pill. The secretary helps her drink the water.

RITA *(The panic momentarily over):* You got any sleeping pills there?

THE SECRETARY: Yeah.

RITA: Maybe I ought to take one of those too.

THE SECRETARY: Okay.

The secretary goes to her large bag on the chest of drawers and takes out a larger bottle and starts to unscrew the cap. A quick look of cunning crosses Rita's face.

RITA: Why don't you go down and tell my husband to come on up? I'll take the pill after he goes. Then I could sleep on the plane.

THE SECRETARY *(Screwing the cap back on and returning the bottle to her bag):* Okay. You want a sandwich?

RITA: That'll be fine.

The secretary goes out of the bedroom, Rita watching her with sly caution. After a moment, Rita gets out of the bed and looks out the doorway and then moves quickly on her bare feet to her secretary's bag, filches the bottle of sleeping pills, and moves back to her bed, putting the bottle under her pillow. She sits patiently now, dominated by some feeling of immense achievement, deeply calm. She seems unaware of muffled footsteps on the stairs outside. Tower comes a few tentative steps into the room.

TOWER: Hello, Emmy.

She smiles briefly at him, almost as if she didn't know who he was, as if her mind was on other, more profoundly moving things.

RITA: I was just thinking that life is really a fraud, isn't it? There's really nothing to it at all. I'm thirty-one years old, and I look back on it all, and all I feel like saying is "So what?" I think of all that heartache and fretting—

TOWER: Slings and arrows . . .

RITA: I got a handsome house with gardens as far as your eye can see, filled with red flowers of paradise and tulips. And I can hardly get out of a taxicab in New York but there's hundreds of people crowding around the door, screaming how much they love me. I've known men, hundreds of men, just blank faces—I can't remember them at all. I don't believe there's anything in this world I haven't tried once. All the things that are supposed to be fun really ain't no fun, and all the things that are supposed to be important really ain't nothing at all. For the life of me, I can't think of any reason to get up tomorrow morning. I can't think of anything I want or look forward to. It's all a fraud, isn't it, John?

TOWER: No.

She lies back on the bed and looks up at the ceiling, quiet with an almost drunken feeling of omnipotent knowledge.

RITA: Why, I remember you, drunk as sin in that dirty little room in the Hotel Montgomery, shouting these very things at me, quoting all the great poets.

TOWER: "All life is weariness," saith the preacher. "No man can utter it."

RITA: I remember when I was a little girl I used to dream of drowning all the time.

TOWER: "The dark tideless floods of nothingness, where all who know may drown."

RITA (*Staring up at the ceiling*): That seems to me an awful nice feeling, to just float and let the water come up over you, for I can't bear this life no more. I can't. You wouldn't understand.

TOWER: Sure I would.

There is something so gentle in his voice that she looks at him. He is regarding her with great sweetness.

RITA: How have you been, John? I never did get to talk to you too much the last time we met.

TOWER: Oh, still in one piece.

RITA: How kind you look!

TOWER: I was just thinking you're so unchanged. I wish I were meeting you now for the first time.

She is suddenly pressing herself against him, her face against his chest.

RITA: Hold me, John.

He holds her gently.

RITA: I never loved anybody but you.

TOWER (*Holding her gently*): You never loved me either, Emmy. You needed me, but you never loved me. You never knew what love was. Whoever taught it to you?

She is crying, and he holds her, caught himself in a surge of emotion.

TOWER: Life is unbearable if you don't love something, Emmy. Don't I know that as well as you? Come with me now. Put on your clothes and come with me. The girl is waiting at the bottom of the hill. I want you to meet her. People like us can never love anything but our children. But that's something. She's given me moments of great pleasure—moments when I can see that life is fine. She wants to meet you so much.

RITA *(Face pressed against his chest):* I can't. I can't!

TOWER: That's the reason we came down here, because she wanted to meet you so much.

RITA *(In panic):* I can't face her! She despises me!

TOWER: Emmy . . .

RITA *(Flinging herself away from him):* Leave me alone!

From the open doorway of the bedroom we hear the secretary's voice:

THE SECRETARY: Leave her alone.

Tower turns to look at the secretary.

RITA *(In full panic):* I'm no good! I'm no good!

TOWER *(To the secretary):* Would you rather she clutches at life for half hours in cheap hotel rooms?

RITA *(Sobbing):* I had my mother in labor for seventeen hours and I been nothing but pain to everybody since!

THE SECRETARY *(Moving to her):* Rita . . .

RITA: Leave me alone.

THE SECRETARY *(To Rita):* Give me the bottle. Where'd you put it?

RITA: Leave me alone.

THE SECRETARY: Where'd you put the bottle of sleeping pills, Rita?

RITA: Save me, save me, save me!

The secretary slaps her sharply, and the panic subsides as abruptly as it began. Rita stands in the middle of the room, her hair awry, fingering her long white nightgown. Tower regards her with deep, pained compassion. The secretary caresses her hair gently.

THE SECRETARY (*Kindly*): Where's the bottle, baby?

RITA (*Murmuring*): Under the pillow.

The secretary leans over the bed and extracts the bottle of sleeping pills from under the pillow.

THE SECRETARY: Lie down, baby. I have a sandwich for you outside.

Rita moves silently, like a punished child, to the bed and lies down. The secretary shuffles to Tower and looks at him in an oddly pleading way.

THE SECRETARY (*To Tower*): We got her to a psychiatrist for four months. Then he said to me we were wasting our money. She's a dead woman, emotionally dead. She could keep coming every day for an hour and pour out her heart, and this would relieve the immediate tensions, but she would never really respond to treatment. I'll take her back to California, and she'll go on making movies, because that's all she knows to do, and whatever happens after that happens. But I kind of love her, and I'll take good care of her.

TOWER: All right. *(He smiles at Rita)* I'll see you, Emmy.

RITA *(Smiling from the bed):* Please call me if you get out to the Coast.

TOWER: Of course. *(He turns and goes out onto the landing)*

INTERIOR. *The landing outside the bedroom.* FULL SHOT *of Tower going down the stairs.*

EXTERIOR. *The street outside the aunt's home. Night.* FULL SHOT *of Tower coming out of the house, going down the walk and out to the sidewalk. He begins to walk quickly down the hill. There is a feeling of pain and urgency and deeply stirred emotions in Tower.*

CLOSE SHOT *across Tower's shoulders as he reaches the bottom of the hill where it joins Main Street. There is an ice-cream parlor sandwiched between several other stores facing him across the street. Standing in the lighted doorway is his daughter. He stops and stares at the girl, his face almost bursting with the pain of his love for her. Then he comes to her, takes her hand, and leads her briskly farther down Main Street to the little jumble of lights that constitutes the heart of town.*

TOWER: She never had a chance, honey. She never had a chance from the beginning.

They go off down the dark hill into the scattering of lights in the heart of town. Soon they are swallowed up in the darkness.

FADE OUT.

About the Author

PADDY CHAYEFSKY *was born in New York City on January 29, 1923. He attended DeWitt Clinton High School and City College before enlisting in the Army during World War II. In Germany he ran afoul of a booby trap that put him in the hospital, where, while convalescing, he wrote the book and lyrics for the Army musical* No T. O. for Love. *After the war and a brief experience in his uncle's print shop, he turned to writing scripts for radio, television, movies and, finally, the stage.* Television Plays, *a collection of his best dramas, was published in 1955. He is also the author of the Broadway hit* Middle of the Night. *Mr. Chayefsky is married and lives in Manhattan.*

5¢F
2/~~100~~

35¢
3/~~100~~